FANTASTIC
PLASTIC

FANTASTIC PLASTIC

product design + consumer culture

black dog
publishing
london uk

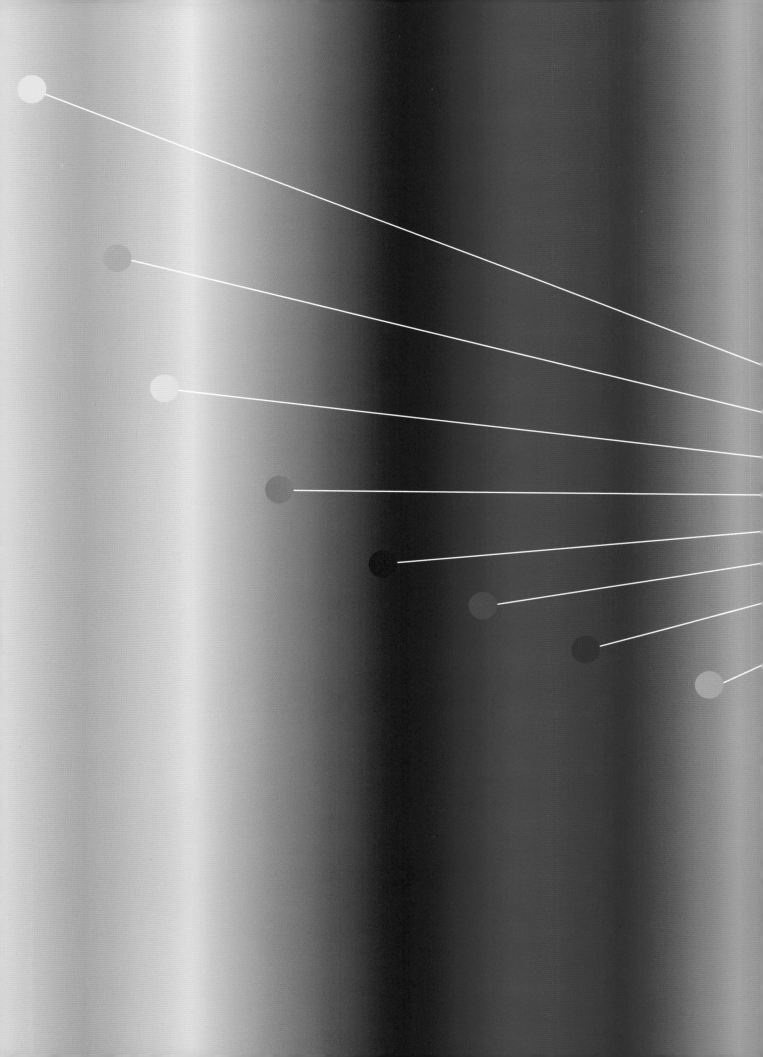

CONTENTS

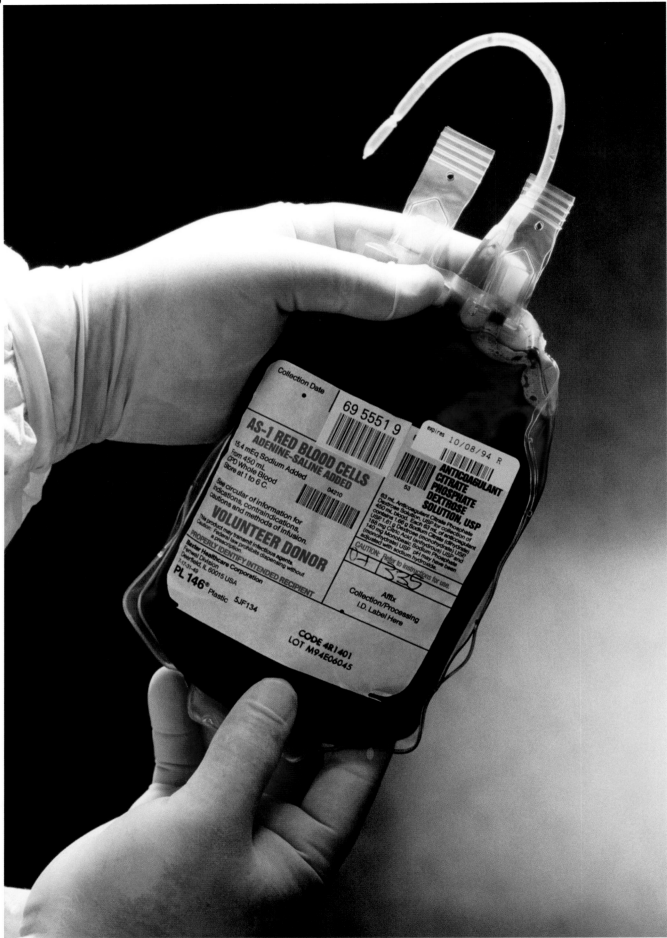

We live in a world of plastic—both literally and figuratively. Plastics are materials we see everywhere on a daily basis—from the moment we brush our teeth with a plastic toothbrush in the morning and tie our plastic laces before going to school or work, until we climb into nylon pyjamas and brush our teeth with that brush again. We understand plastics as materials that embrace a whole range of forms, functions, colours and feel. As consumers we may wear plastic clothes, drive a plastic car, and even eat using plastic utensils. If we need a spare body part, we may also be given a plastic heart valve or vein—even our dentures are plastic.

The word "plastics" can evoke strong responses in people—they may love it, and even dream of it, or they may despise it.

Plastics play a contradictory role in the twenty-first century—they can save lives in the form of PVC blood bags or can despoil the landscape, evident when plastics rubbish is disposed of carelessly, taking years to decompose. Plastics can be mass-produced or hand-fabricated and either low cost or very expensive. The philosopher, Roland Barthes, called plastics "a miraculous substance... a transformation of nature".

DESIGN

Plastics have been used to make iconic objects and design classics such as the iPod and the Tulip Chair. They are now invisible, ubiquitous in high-tech applications, such as the casings for mobile phones and personal computers, or in the bodies of military and civilian aircraft. At the other end of their product design range, they have been used to make what may be perceived as cheap and tacky goods that are disposable or break easily.

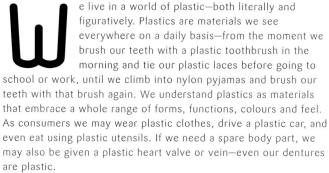

8

UNDERSTANDING PLASTIC

At the beginning of the twentieth century, when they were first introduced, there was no real understanding of plastics, the notion of their convenience or their application. With the advent of Bakelite in 1907, invented by Leo Baekeland, it took several years for this new synthetic plastic to be recognised as a material in its own right and that good design would be integral to plastics' success. Early Bakelite was often produced in a form that imitated wood but cast phenolic, a plastic developed in 1928, liberated this material from its "woody roots", and Bakelite was produced in colours that imitated amber or jade. Important designers, such as Raymond Loewy and Walter Teague in America, and Wells Wintemute Coates and Serge Chermaeyeff in Britain, embraced this new material in the 1930s and took it to new heights. Their design ethos was strengthened in Britain by the setting up of groups such as the Industrial Design Partnership in 1935 and the Design Research Unit in 1943.

As early as the First World War, shortages of raw materials led to some European manufacturers making cheap imitations of phenolic plastics (Bakelite). These shoddy imitations did not perform as well as Bakelite itself but were still perceived as part of the range of plastics on the market. This misperception may have been a contributory factor to the resistance of the German-based Bauhaus school to the use of these new materials in architecture and furniture in the 1920s and 30s. The Bauhaus ethos favoured traditional wood or metals. However, even this severe design school had exponents who used plastics to make what have now become classic designs. These include important designers such as Gaby Schreiber, an Austrian Second World War refugee to Britain, who designed a range of plastics tableware.

TACKY PLASTIC?

The cheap and tacky perception of plastics, which was current particularly in the 1950s, but has continued in some areas until the present day, may be partially a result of the glut of plastics after the end of the Second World War. This sometimes led to the inappropriate plastic being used for a particular application and also certain manufacturers and/or designers ignoring some of the inherent weaknesses of the plastic concerned. For example, early polystyrene was inherently brittle and was often used to make

BOTTOM LEFT: The Rubik's Cube is a mechanical plastic puzzle invented in 1974 by Hungarian sculptor and professor of architecture, Ern Rubik. Originally called the Magic Cube the puzzle is said to be the world's best-selling toy, with over 300,000,000 Rubik's Cubes and imitations sold worldwide.

BOTTOM RIGHT: Advertised as a stress relieving pen holder, Dead Fred's silicone rubber body is strong enough to hold pens, and to retain its shape after the pen has been removed. The design allows Fred to be stabbed by a pen multiple times, thus alleviating stress for the user. Dead Fred was designed by Yann Le Bouedec.

OPPOSITE: Mannequins can be made from polystyrene or fibreglass. Polystyrene mannequins are cheaper to manufacture, and lighter to transport. Fibreglass is the preferred material for designers, as paint adheres well to fibreglass and the mannequin can be modified with paint should the consumer require a different look. Fibreglass mannequins can also be constructed with fabricated joints to permit some posing and articulation in the joints.

THE COMMON DICTIONARY DEFINITION OF PLASTICS IS A "MATERIAL CAPABLE OF BEING MOULDED"

10

mass-produced toys. Such examples of polystyrene toys, imported from Hong Kong and Taiwan, developed a reputation for breaking easily. However, this property of brittleness in polystyrene was later modified by adding another plastic polymer. This new, high impact polystyrene could withstand an impact seven times that of ordinary polystyrene, and is widely used for packaging and for more resilient toys today.

In the 1940s, it appears that the general public still did not understand these new materials and treated plastics in the same way as they would have treated items made of more traditional materials, such as metal. Tales are told of plastic colanders being put over a hot saucepan or polythene washing up bowls being put before an open fire and melting. Such occurrences made people suspicious of these new materials and gave plastics a bad name.

So when did we become aware of plastics as such? In the nineteenth century, before the first truly synthetic plastics were made, plastics, as a collective noun for a material, did not exist, though the quality of a material being plastic and mouldable was understood. Hence, natural materials such as rubber and horn were 'plastic', in that they could be moulded and shaped under heat and pressure. By the mid-nineteenth century people were looking for substitutes for natural materials, such as ivory and tortoiseshell, which were becoming increasingly rare. Parkesine, based on cellulose nitrate, and developed in the 1850s, was a precursor of Celluloid. This latter material became a convincing substitute for natural ivory and tortoiseshell.

It was not until the twentieth century and the advent of Bakelite, the first truly synthetic material, that this group of materials—plastics—began to be recognised as a category in their own right. The common dictionary definition of plastics is a material, "capable of being moulded". In 1926, the adjective plastic was defined in the American trade magazine, *Plastics*, as: "The property of a substance by virtue of which it can be formed or moulded into any desired shape, as opposed to non-plastic substances which must be cut or chiselled." The definition of plastics as a material was described, by the plastics historian, J Harry DuBois, as "any material that by its nature or in its process of manufacture is at some stage, either through heat or by the presence of a solvent, sufficiently pliable and flowable, in other words plastic, so that it can be given its final shape by the operation of moulding or pressing".

As early as 1941, in their book, *Plastics* (later reprinted as *Plastics in the Service of Man*), chemists Dr VE Yarsley and EG Couzens foretold a 'Plastics Age'. The Victoria & Albert Museum mounted an exhibition of the same name in 1990, curated by cultural historian Penny Sparke, a noted design expert. Dr Victor Emmanuel Yarsley OBE specialised in cellulose acetate and organic polymers. Edward Gordon Couzens OBE, specialised in explosives and later thermoplastics and photographic film. Both were fellows

of the Plastics Institute (now part of the Institute of Materials, Minerals and Mining). Professor Penny Sparke is a specialist in late nineteenth and twentieth century design history, professor Sparke edited *The Plastics Age: From Modernity to Postmodernity*, 1990, and her other publications include: *An Introduction to Design and Culture in the Twentieth Century*; *A Century of Design: Pioneers of the Twentieth Century* and *Italian Design: 1870 to the Present*.

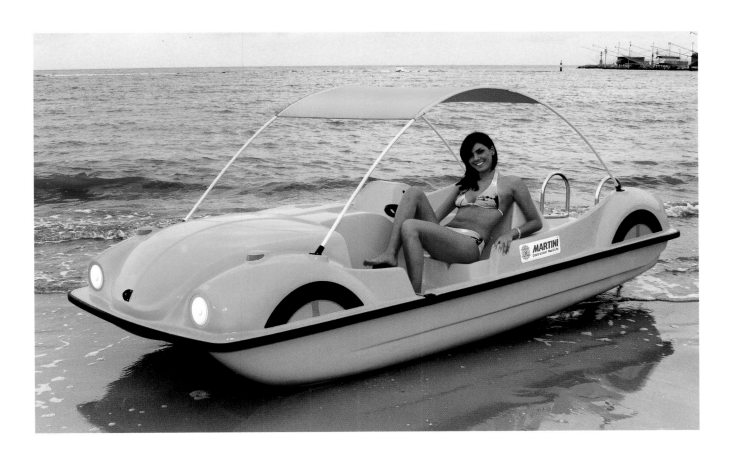

OPPOSITE: Inflatable PVC stool, circa 1954, by Verner Panton. Panton is considered one of Denmark's most influential twentieth century furniture and interior designers. During his career, he created innovative and futuristic designs in a variety of materials, but is arguably most remembered for his work with plastics. Panton's designs were typically 1960s in style, but regained popularity at the end of the twentieth century. As of 2004, Panton's most recognisable furniture models are still in production.

BOTTOM: Construction workers' protective polyethylene hard hat. Safety helmets were originally made from metal, then fibreglass until the 1950s, when rigid thermoplastic, such as ABS, became widely available. Polyethylene is now used as a protective material in a wide variety of applications throughout the world.

THE WORD "PLASTICS" CAN EVOKE STRONG RESPONSES IN PEOPLE— THEY MAY LOVE IT, AND EVEN DREAM OF IT, OR THEY MAY DESPISE IT

EMERGING
CONSUMER
MARKETS

Bakelite's inventor, Leo Baekeland, immediately recognised that there would be many uses for his product, although initially he concentrated on commercial applications in the electrical, automotive and military industries. The poor wartime imitations of phenolic plastics had led to a negative public perception of plastics after the First World War. Allan Brown, who became the Bakelite Corporation's advertising and public relations director, 1921, recognised that something needed to be done to improve the public image of Bakelite. Brown had the insight to realise that the female market could be major consumers of domestic Bakelite products and were worth addressing in their own right. Brown organised the advertising booklet, *A Romance of Industry*, specifically designed to attract the female customer. The process of the mythologising of Bakelite to emphasise its importance and "infinite" uses was also Brown's brainchild. His next action was to commission the book, *The Story of Bakelite*, by journalist, John Kimberly Mumford. This 1924 publication used florid prose and hyperbole to describe the invention of Bakelite and its importance to the world, which he links to the story of creation. Mumford calls Bakelite "wonder-stuff". He goes on to write "Heat—and yet more heat—wrought the miracle", and describes Bakelite as "a contradiction, a mystery, a tireless factotum—a triumph of creative chemistry" claiming that "The fairy-godmother... bestowed so many gifts on Bakelite."

Contemporary advertising booklets called Bakelite: "oxybenzylmethylenglycolanhydride or modern magic", a statement intended to reiterate plastic's complexity and simplicity.[1] When Baekeland developed Bakelite in 1907, there was no clear understanding of the concept of giant molecules. This was the work of Hermann Staudinger after the First World War and in the 1920s, and later that of Wallace Carothers and his team at DuPont in the 1930s. However, Staudinger's theory of macromolecules was not generally accepted until the mid-1930s. Prior to this the view was that polymers were made up of aggregates of smaller molecules.

A CONTRADICTION, A MYSTERY, A TIRELESS FACTOTUM—A TRIUMPH OF CREATIVE CHEMISTRY

John Mumford

Recognising the importance of good design, Allan Brown initiated a series of design seminars, the first in January 1933, and signed up key designers for a series of advertisements. This campaign ensured that the best American designers, including Norman Bel Geddes and Raymond Loewy, designed and promoted Bakelite objects. By 1938, the Bakelite Corporation had produced their landmark film, *The Fourth Kingdom*, designed to put Bakelite on the world stage. The Bakelite Corporation were equating their product with the universally acknowledged kingdoms of animals, vegetables and minerals—Bakelite and its products were suggested to be from a kingdom in their own right, with unlimited boundaries. In 1938, Brown also organised a Bakelite Travelcade, designed as a touring exhibition on "Modern Plastics for Modern Living", to stimulate public demand.

By the 1930s, then, the plastics industry was reaching new levels of confidence on both sides of the Atlantic and plastics themselves were really being brought to the public's attention, with trade shows, exhibitions and vigorous advertising campaigns. A series of popular exhibitions showcased those plastics then available. In addition to Bakelite and the cellulosic plastics—such as cellulose nitrate (Celluloid) and cellulose acetate—there were also the thioureas and urea formaldehydes, used for a range of decorative goods including picnic sets, and glorifying in trade names such as "Bandalasta" and "Beetle". Also with the phenolic resins and urea formaldehydes came a range of laminates, the first of which was Formica. Dating back to as early as 1912, such laminates were swiftly used for luxurious interiors, including the ocean liner, The Queen Mary. The urea formaldehyde laminates and the later melamine formaldehyde laminates, developed in the 1930s, offered washable, convenient and colourful surfaces and also fed into the relaxed cafe culture which developed after the Second World War as prosperity returned to Britain and America in the 1950s and 60s.

THE POLY ERA

The 1930s were a very significant period for the development of plastics. This could be called the "poly" era as polythene, polymethyl methacrylate (Perspex); polyamide (nylon), polystyrene, polyvinyl chloride (PVC) and polyurethane (PU) came on the scene. When war broke out in 1939, the major output of these new plastics went into the war effort—nylon made parachutes and polythene was used to insulate radar cables. Nylon stockings became so precious that American GIs posted to Britain were reputed to trade them for sexual favours.

PLASTIC DURING THE WAR

During the war, new plastics were also developed, notably PTFE (otherwise known as Teflon by DuPont in America), and polyester, in the form of Terylene fibres, in Britain. Polyester, and later epoxy

resins, became very important in the development of composites such as glass reinforced fibre (GRP) in the late 1940s.

America had already developed a form of synthetic rubber called Duprene in 1931, later called Neoprene in 1936. In Germany, scientists had been working on developing synthetic rubber from 1906. Working initially on variations of isoprene, the German company Bayer (which later merged to create IG Farbenindustrie), patented styrene-butadiene (Buna S) in 1929 and butadiene-acrylonitrile (Buna N) in 1930. Buna S was then developed further to compete with the American plastics, and to make the German Reich independent of rubber supplied by Malaysia, as the Malaysian rubber industry was controlled before and during the Second World War by the British, with the British Navy implementing blockades to stop this material reaching Germany. Germany started to produce commercial synthetic rubbers, Buna S and Buna N, in 1937. Although IG Farbenindustrie was collaborating with the American Standard Oil Company, New Jersey, once Pearl Harbour was bombed in 1941 the Americans were drawn into the war and such relations ceased. America then developed government rubber-styrene (GR-S) which resembled Germany's Buna-S recipe, but, in fact, ended up outperforming it.

By 1945, the military need for plastics was abated with the end of the war, and a new range of plastics became available to the public. New markets needed to be discovered for these materials and British companies, such as ICI, had a surplus of polythene because it was no longer needed to insulate radar cables as part of the war effort. Companies searched for bright new ideas for products utilising the new plastic material. The late 1940s and early 1950s saw a range of consumer polythene products developed. These included products designed for long term use, such as the polythene washing bowl (which replaced metal enamelled bowls), children's dolls and, of course, Tupperware, the brainchild of American Earl, Silas Tupper.

CONSTIPATED
LITTLE OBJECTS

Paul Reilly

TUPPERWARE

A former employee of DuPont, engineer and entrepreneur Earl Tupper manipulated polythene waste to produce his own 'Poly-T' polythene. This he called: "Poly-T the material of the future", and Tupper was keen to find a use for it. Inspired by his wife's complaints about the difficulty of storing food in the fridge, Tupper came up with the brilliant concept of a snap-top polythene container. When being closed, and air expelled, this closure emitted what became known as the "Tupperware burp". The success of Tupperware may be attributed to the ability to seal the containers and this must have been due to very accurate dimensional tolerances of the moulds for matching components plus careful tool maintenance to maintain the tolerances.

This was the beginning of the Tupperware empire, spurred on by the marketing genius of the company's marketing guru, Brownie Wise. Tupperware was sold in homes—by housewives to other housewives—and the Tupperware party became synonymous with visions of the ideal American housewife of the 1950s and 60s, immortalised in colourful contemporary adverts. The success of Tupperware relied on innovative, well-designed products and successful marketing. The Tupperware party reached Britain and became popular in the 1960s. Still successful today, it was revealed that even Queen Elizabeth II of Britain uses Tupperware.

OPPOSITE: Tupperware advertising, circa 1960. The Tupperware Company pioneered a direct marketing strategy, utilised by Brownie Wise, and made famous by parties where women showcased Tupperware in the comfort of their own homes. An example of the longevity of Tupperware's popularity is the fact that, even in 2008,Tupperware Brands Corporation was ranked second on *Fortune* magazine's coveted Most Admired Household Products list. Tupperware is still sold mostly through the company's social party plan and parties can also take place in workplaces, schools, and other community groups.

BOTTOM: Game-playing at a Tupperware party, circa 1950. Courtesy of Getty Images.

PLASTIC DESIGN

By the 1950s there was a whole range of more ephemeral polythene products. In 1951 the first blow-moulded packaging was produced, including the Jif lemon and the Vinolia Teddy bear. 1956 saw the production of the disposable polystyrene Bic biro and, by 1959, the iconic PVC Barbie doll also appeared, which became the beloved toy of so many little girls. The Barbie franchise is now a major industry with a range of associated products targeted at young girls. The term "Barbie" is currently used as an adjective to describe a particularly plasticky and 'pneumatic' type of female— the reverse of natural. The 1950s also saw the first plastic bag, an item which continues to inspire debate today.

In parallel with these smaller consumer products—dolls and food storage solutions—the new plastics were eagerly embraced by a new generation of furniture designers after 1945, with an important consumer market developing as a consequence. Key to this area was the advent of reinforced glass fibre composites. These materials liberated designers' imaginations to make new, organic forms in boat, car and furniture design. Charles Eames' one-piece classic fibreglass chair, La Chaise, 1948, illustrates this new way of thinking about form and manufacture. This freer approach is also strongly reflected in Finnish designer, Eero Saarinen's Tulip table and chair set of 1955–1956, produced by Knoll. In the 1950s Italian designers had a significant influence on the development of plastic furniture design. In 1966, Vico Magistretti designed the Selene dining chair in acrylonitrile butadiene styrene (ABS), produced by Artemide. Other Italian companies, such as Pirelli and Kartell, were particularly significant in terms of product design at the time. The work of the Kartell factory, under the direction of Giulio Castelli (who co-founded the Kartell company and was trained as a chemical engineer under Guilio Natta), was a very important contributor to this new design ethos. Kartell produced classics such as the K4999 high-density polythene chair, designed by Marco Zanuso in 1967, and the 4867 chair, made of ABS, designed by Joe Columbo in 1968. Columbo's

4867 chair was the first industrial seat to be injected into a single mould rather than several sections. Columbo's one-piece stackable seat, Universale chair 4860, was originally made of ABS and is now made of polypropylene.

Despite the emerging plastic design ethos in Europe, in Britain there was some resistance to plastics. This was partly due to a dislike by established Arts bodies, including the Council of Industrial Design (CoIM), the Arts Council and the BBC. The worry was that with plastics came a suffocating abundance of mass-produced mass-culture and excess Americanisation, which conflicted with British heritage. In 1950, Paul Reilly, of CoIM, called plastics, "constipated little objects". He also said: "it is this very ease of processing which so often leads to trouble and... tastelessness". In Evelyn Waugh's 1957 book, *The Ordeal of Gilbert Pinfold*, the main character, Pinfold, is described as abhorring "plastics, Picasso, sunbathing and jazz—everything in fact that had happened in his own lifetime".

In the 1960s, designers' imaginations knew no bounds, and produced surprising new designs in PVC. The PVC Blow Chair was designed in 1967 by Scolari, Lomazzi, D'Urbino and de Pas. The chair was produced almost in a spirit of anti-design and, according to cultural historian, Penny Sparke in 1990, deliberately used soft,

IT IS THIS VERY EASE OF PROCESSING WHICH SO OFTEN LEADS TO TROUBLE AND... TASTELESSNESS

Paul Reilly of CoIM

flexible plastics that opposed the nature of sturdy design. Other startling designs include the inflatable Cushicle—a PVC tubular relaxing space showcased at the Milan Triennale in 1968. This era of inflatable PVC is perhaps best personified by the vision of a naked Barbarella reclining in her PVC tunnel in the eponymous cult film of the same name.

A reflection of plastic culture was also seen in the 1967 film, *The Graduate*, when the businessman, Mr McGuire, declares to Dustin Hoffman: "I just want to say one word to you—just one word—'plastics'." Although this statement is amusing in the context of the film, outside in the real world plastics were changing ideas about design in a profound way.

PLASTIC FASHION

Fashion designers were also using PVC as a high fashion material. In 1963, Mary Quant created her Wet Look collection, which epitomised the dolly bird look of the 1960s and caused a sensation. French couture fashion designers, André Courrèges and Pierre Cardin, created the classic space age PVC fashion, with PVC mini-dresses accessorised with boots, perhaps reflecting and/or influencing the look of the contemporary film, *2001: A Space Odyssey*, 1968. Unfortunately, due to the nature of early PVC, the iconic furniture and fashion items made from the material in the 1960s are now a problem for museums and collectors as they ooze plasticisers, discolour, distort and crack. Perhaps this is why the influx of inflatable furniture in the 1990s became so prevalent and popular, as people remembered the ephemeral nature of the Blow Chair and the constant sense of fun that came with PVC merchandise. However, contemporary 1960s accounts tell us that as the furniture deflated— stubbed by cigarettes, placed on pins, accidentally stabbed—the limited shelf life of the furniture was realised.

Modern PVC is quite a different animal. Resistant to water, this plastic is now the choice for over 60 per cent of the European population for their window frames, and a particular favourite in Germany. PVC window frames may be anathema to architectural purists, but they do not suffer from dry rot as wood does, and now may even be made from recycled PVC, which is less destructive to the environment.

POLYURETHANE FOAMS

Polyurethane foams became key to a range of new furniture designs in the 1960s, from the G-Plan furniture launched in 1963, to the Djinn chairs made of polyurethane foam designed by Olivier Mourgue, in 1965. Roberto Matta's Malitte Lounge Furniture from 1966, and extraordinary pieces, such as Nani Prina's Sculpture sofa and Roger Dean's body shape-adapting Sea Urchin Chair of 1968, were created during the decade. 1969 saw the arrival of the Sacco Bean Bag, which contained polyurethane pellets in a PVC sack and was designed by Piero Gatti, Cesare Paolini and Franco

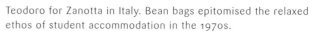

Teodoro for Zanotta in Italy. Bean bags epitomised the relaxed ethos of student accommodation in the 1970s.

The early 1970s saw furniture production increase by 60 per cent. Astonishing experimental seating was designed with a Pop art flavour, and made from polyurethane foam and Dacron padding. In 1970, De Pas, D'Urbino, and Lomazzi produced the baseball-shaped Joe armchair for Poltronova. Design Studio 65 dreamt up the bright red lips sofa, Bocca. In 1971 Gruppo Strum designed the Big Meadow (Pratone) armchair that resembled a swatch of grass. Living room seating had become less structured and could be used in a variety of ways.

Plastic domestic appliances received the Italian designer treatment, including the nylon Spalter vacuum cleaner, designed in 1956 by Achille and Pier Giacomo Castiglioni, for the Italian Company, REM. The designers intended this cleaner to be carried like a bag, slung across the vacuumer's back with a leather strap. Achille Castiglioni had the maxim: "Start from scratch. Stick to common sense. Know your goals and means."

PLASTIC ARCHITECTURE

Milan Polytechnic University trained many of Italy's key architects and designers, numbers of whom continued to be leaders in architecture and product design for several decades, some even into the twenty-first century. The Italian Association for Industrial

THE DESIGNER'S COMMON AIM WAS TO BUILD A MORE RATIONAL, PLEASANT AND BEAUTIFUL HUMAN SOCIETY, EVEN WITH REGARD TO ITS MINOR ASPECTS, SUCH AS A TELEVISION OR AN ALARM CLOCK

Giovanni Albera and Nicholas Monti

OPPOSITE: Artist, Jackson Pollock, using his 'drip' technique. Pollock's iconic images required a paint with fluid viscosity and he used the then new synthetic resin-based paints, called acrylic alkyd enamels to achieve this. Photograph by Martha Holmes. Courtesy of Getty Images.

Design (ADI) was founded in 1956, with Achille Castiglioni being a founder member. In the book *Italian Modern: A Design Heritage*, 1989, Giovanni Albera and Nicholas Monti commented that "The designer's common aim [was] to build a more rational, pleasant and beautiful human society, even with regard to its minor aspects, such as a television or an alarm clock." There was no distinction made between the terms "architect" and "designer", and the term "industrial designer" was not used as a unique occupation title until the end of the twentieth century. The educational training of these people was usually from a school of architecture, such as Milan Polytechnic University. Triennale exhibitions in Milan were a key element in promulgating these new designs. In Milan, Stile Industria and Materie Plastiche presented the first Aesthetic of Plastics International Exhibition, at the XXXIV Campionaria Fair.

By the 1980s, German designer Dieter Rams was designing a range of plastic housings for a variety of electrical and electronic household devices for Braun including hairdryers, electric shavers, and tooth brushes which were masterpieces of artistic and functional design. Rams had a very deep understanding of the possibilities of very accurate injection moulding of different polymers for different functions and how to use tight tolerances to good effect in snap fitting, moulded switches and other applications. Alternatively, Argentinian designer Daniel Weil was to put an almost abstract twist on the design of a simple radio, which he placed in a welded PVC envelope, produced by Parenthesis in 1981.

PLASTIC ART

American artists including Roy Lichtenstein and Jackson Pollock used acrylic house paints as early as the 1940s. Pollock commented in 1950 that: "new needs need new techniques". Artists in Britain were slower to adopt these less traditional materials, but by the 1950s, Jon Cautleugh, Denis Bowen and Patrick Heron were also using plastics in their work—perhaps for reasons of lower cost rather than aesthetics.[2]

On a more everyday note, the house owner and do-it-yourself enthusiast is now helped by a range of increasingly quick drying and user-friendly synthetic paints that do not need thinners and can be washed out of brushes with water, rather than chemicals.

NEW NEEDS NEED NEW TECHNIQUES

Jackson Pollock

Opposite: Naum Gabo's plastic sculpture, *Linear Construction Number Two 2*, at Tate, London. From left to right, Barbara Hepworth, Naum Gabo, Henry Moore and Lady Read. The piece consists of a light-catching nylon filament, which is wound around two intersecting acrylic sheet planes. The stringing gives a delicate sense of three dimensions in the complicated patterns created by the irregular lobe shapes of the transparent plastic. Photograph by Douglas Miller. Courtesy of Getty Images.

BELOW: David Olschewski's Waterwings stool. Olschewski places objects in different contexts, thus supplying the object with a new purpose than that intended. In this design eight PVC water wings are used to make the seat to the stool. Stability is lent to the construction by rods which are connected to the stool's acrylic legs.

PLASTIC SCULPTURE

Sculptors used plastics from an early period. In the 1920s Naum Gabo used cellulose nitrate and cellulose acetate sheet in his early Constructivist sculptures. This utilisation of materials is increasingly problematic for the museums and collectors that now own these artworks, as these particular plastics are very sensitive to light and heat and prone to degradation, sometimes in a very short period. Later Gabo also used nylon and acrylic (Perspex) alongside traditional materials, such as wood. With the multitude of materials available to artists, it is questionable why Gabo used plastics. One factor may have been an appreciation of their properties, such as transparency and ease of working. Artist Patrick Heron commented in 1953 that Gabo "chooses the most neutral, most nearly non-existent material to hand, an almost invisible plastic, as devoid of quality or personality as any material could be". On the other hand, Gabo may have simply used what was readily available and affordable, as well as quick and easy to work with. At Tate, London, efforts are being made to make computerised virtual copies of Gabo's most fragile cellulosic plastics sculptures, so that even if the originals become distorted and warped beyond recognition, at least a virtual form may survive for future generations.

PLASTIC EXTERIORS

Architects were slower to apply plastics in their design work and those who did adopted adventurous approaches, whether by using plastics sheeting as an inflatable material—as became the approach taken by British company, Inflate—or designed as impermanent or deployable structures—found in the work of the German architect, Frei Otto. More recently the roof of the Millennium Dome in Greenwich, London, is made of PTFE (Teflon) coated glass fibre fabric.

PLASTIC INTERIORS

Plastic laminates—ranging from phenolic, and urea-formaldehyde-based materials, to melamine-based plastics—were used in commercial and domestic interiors. The most notable of these is Formica, made from a range of different plastics and in different finishes and colours. Formica laminate was used to make the glossy interiors in Hollywood films and promoted an idea of glamour. At the other end of the scale, Fablon, a PVC sticky-backed plastic, came on the market in the 1970s and was available in a variety of colours and patterns, and was used for wallpaper as well as for protecting surfaces. Design purists widely detested this material.

At the extreme end of giant-but-disposable plastics is the work of Christo and Jeanne-Claude—the contemporary artists known for wrapping polypropylene or nylon sheet around existing landmarks, including Greek and Roman statues, and government buildings across the world. The Kunsthalle, Bern, Switzerland, the Pont Neuf, Paris, and the Reichstag, Berlin, are noted examples of buildings wrapped in plastic by the duo, and they have even wrapped entire landscapes in nylon sheet.

At another end of the spectrum polythene sheeting is extensively used to make temporary tunnels for gardening and crop management. However, this has also been seen as non-conducive to the beauty of the environment—despite polythene's practical and economic aspects for protecting and enhancing crop growth.

1. Incidentally, by referring to it as oxybenzylmethylenglycolanhydride Baekeland was not quite accurate in this assessment of the chemical structure of Bakelite, which is actually phenol formaldehyde—the modern chemical name for phenol formaldehyde is polyoxybenzylmethylenglycolanhydride. The prefix of poly is representative of several atoms being combined to form the cross-linked molecule.

2. London-based paintings conservator, Harriet Standeven, revealed the low-cost drive in painters' techniques in her Doctoral research examining the use of commercial paints by twentieth century artists.

Plastics are materials which can be formed under heat and pressure, and be made from either natural or synthetic sources. The earliest known plastics are natural materials such as amber, horn, tortoiseshell or natural rubber. Semi-synthetic plastics are partly made from natural materials and partly from chemicals. They include vulcanised rubber, Celluloid and casein. The third category is synthetic plastics which are entirely made from manmade chemicals and include phenol formaldehyde (Bakelite), nylon, polythene, PVC, polystyrene and polypropylene.

Plastics are polymers: substances composed of long chains of repeating molecules (known as monomers) mainly composed of carbon and hydrogen atoms. Under the right conditions these monomers can be made to join up into chain structures. The simplest synthetic polymer is polythene, which has a backbone of carbon atoms attached to hydrogen atoms. One carbon and two hydrogen atoms make up the monomers of polythene. These are joined together to make a chain of atoms (a molecule) in a process called polymerisation. These long chains of atoms are known as polymers.

By organising polymer chains in different ways, or adding different elements to the molecule, it is possible to make new polymers or enhance the properties of the existing polymer. For example, substituting a chlorine atom in a carbon and hydrogen molecule produces the building block for PVC (polyvinyl chloride). Oxygen, nitrogen, chlorine, silicon or other elements may also be found in some other polymers. The long chains of polymer molecules are connected by weak bonds called van der Waals forces.

Other plastics have cross-linked structures with very strong molecular bonds and form thermosetting plastics. These strong chemical bonds give these plastics enhanced heat resistance.

It is also possible to join different types of polymers together in a process called copolymerisation. This is done to enhance the properties of the material produced. An example of a copolymer is acrylonitrile butadiene styrene, in which three different polymers have been joined together to make a tough, impact resistant plastic used for applications such as car bumpers.

Plastics can be divided into two main groups: thermosets and thermoplastics. Thermosetting plastics cannot be melted again once they have been set into shape. These include the phenolic (Bakelite) plastics, urea formaldehydes, melamines and modern composite plastics. They have the advantage of relatively high

PLASTICS ARE MADE UP OF LONG CHAINS OF REPEATING MOLECULES, MAINLY COMPOSED OF CARBON AND HYDROGEN ATOMS

IT IS POSSIBLE
TO JOIN DIFFERENT
TYPES OF POLYMERS
TOGETHER IN A
PROCESS CALLED
COPOLYMERISATION.
THIS IS DONE
TO ENHANCE THE
PROPERTIES OF
THE MATERIAL
PRODUCED

The copolymerisation process
carried out in a labratory, circa
1960.

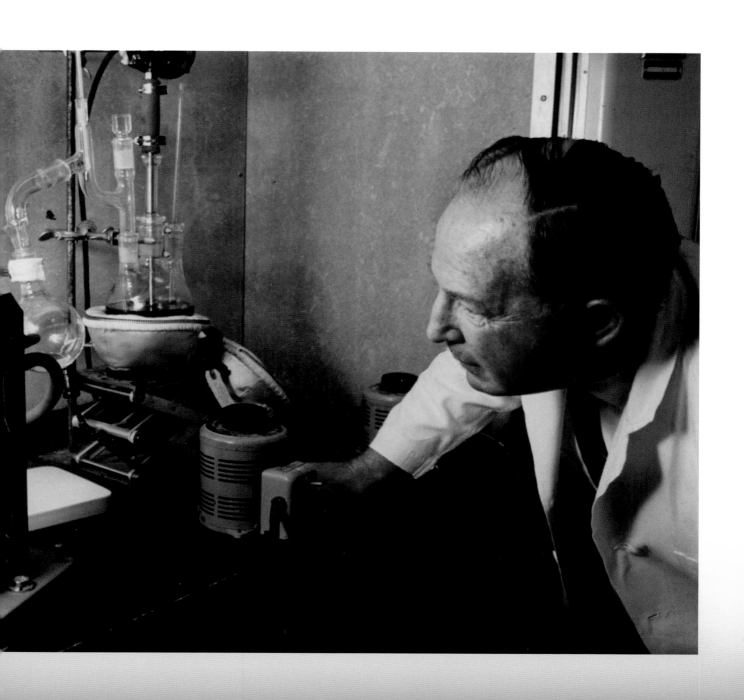

temperature resistance, in terms of plastics—most metals have much higher melting and boiling points. However, in order to recycle thermosets they normally have to be ground down into a powder. This powder can be used again as a filler in a new plastics composite material.

The second group of plastics, thermoplastics, can be melted again after manufacture, and include polythene, PVC, polypropylene and nylon. These plastics have the advantage that they can be sorted, melted and then reused as feed stock to make new plastic products. The key issue with obtaining a good quality product is the need to sort the plastics into the relevant type and to clean them. Mixing different types of thermoplastics together gives a low quality material, dark in colour, which is used for low-end and low-value applications, such as flower pots and park benches. However certain innovative companies are making a range of new laminates which are visually attractive and made from recycled plastics products such as polythene detergent bottles, PVC Wellington boots, crisp packets and even mobile phone casings. One of the biggest sources of recycled plastics is the plastics waste from industrial processing—ideal as the plastic is already sorted by type and is not contaminated with dirt.

The actual structure of plastics was a matter of conjecture and debate in the early years of the twentieth century. In a paper published in 1920, Dr Hermann Staudinger, a German chemist, postulated the existence of giant molecules. However, his views were initially rejected, but in 1953 he was to receive the Nobel Prize for Chemistry for this concept concerning macromolecules.

RAW MATERIALS FOR PLASTICS
In the nineteenth century semi-synthetic plastics were made using natural materials—sometimes cotton flock and cotton fibres—mixed with chemicals—such as nitric and acetic acid. When synthetic plastics were first developed in 1907 with phenolic resins

SOME PLASTICS ARE NOW MADE FROM PLANTS, LIKE SUGAR CANE, STARCH AND CORN, USING PROCESSES SUCH AS BACTERIA OR GENETIC SPLICING, OR FROM BIO FUELS

BOTTOM LEFT: The Wellington boot—also known as a wellie, a topboot, a gumboot, or a rubber boot—is a type of boot based upon Hessian boots. It was worn and popularised by Arthur Wellesley, the first Duke of Wellington and became fashionable among the British aristocracy in the early nineteenth century. Wellington boots are waterproof and are most often made from polyvinyl chloride (PVC). They are usually worn when walking in wet conditions and generally sit just below the knee.

BOTTOM RIGHT: Man wearing gas mask, circa 1920. A gas mask is a mask worn over the face to protect the wearer from inhaling airborne pollutants and toxic materials. The rubber mask forms a sealed cover over the nose and mouth, but may also cover the eyes and other vulnerable soft tissues of the face. Some gas masks are also respirators. The traditional gas mask style with two small circular eye windows originated when the only suitable material for these eye windows was glass. As glass is notoriously brittle, glass eye windows had to be kept small and thick but, later, with the discovery of perspex and then polycarbonate gas masks could have a full face window.

(Bakelite), they were made from products of the coal industry—phenols and formaldehyde. By the 1940s the raw material for plastics had mainly changed to oil and natural gas in America and Britain. The necessary organic chemicals needed to make plastics were distillation products of the petroleum industry.

Today as world stocks of oil are running out, other sources of raw materials for plastics are being explored. Some plastics are now made from plants, like sugar cane, starch and corn, using processes such as bacteria or genetic splicing, or from bio fuels. However, using food crops for fuel or to make plastics is an energy intensive process and is not as environmentally friendly as it might seem at the outset. The dilemma is the economic and ethical ramifications of using food stock to make plastics when there is an increasing world food shortage. There is also an ongoing debate concerning the ethics of genetically engineering food crops as this genetic engineering finally enters the food chain at large.

Another potential future envisages that we find and/or develop alternative sources of fuel for all our industrial needs, such as solar, wind, electric or hydrogen fuel cells. This would, in part, free up more oil to feed the plastics industry. Figures in 2007 indicated that the automotive industry consumed 80 per cent of the world's fossil fuels. Currently plastics use four per cent of the global annual oil output as raw feed stock materials for plastics, and another four per cent of the planet's annual oil is used in the form of energy for the processing and manufacture of plastics.

Another possible approach to the problems of plastics and their sourcing may charm future 'garbologists'—those who excavate landfill sites. The plastics dumped in landfill sites, not decomposing, and so presenting severe environmental problems, might be excavated in the future. These reclaimed plastics could be reused as fuel or potentially even be recycled. However, while the processes to break down plastics into their component building blocks (monomers) have been developed by scientists, plastics experts and industrialists, at present these are not economically viable.

NATURAL
PLASTICS—
KNOWN
SINCE
ANTIQUITY

Horn goblets and drinking horn, circa 1900. Use of animal horns is controversial, especially if the animal is specifically hunted for the horn as a hunting trophy, object of decoration or utility. Some animals are threatened or endangered to reduced populations partially from the pressure of such hunting. Image courtesy of Grays Antiques.

Drinking horns are bovid horns removed from the bone core, cleaned and polished and used as drinking vessels. Powder horns were originally bovid horns fitted with lids and carrying straps, used to carry gunpowder. Horn may be used as a material in tools, furniture and decoration; in these applications, horn is valued for its hardness, and it has given rise to the expression "hard as horn". Horn is somewhat thermoplastic and (like tortoiseshell) was formerly used for many purposes where plastic would now be used.

Natural plastics have been known since antiquity. Bitumen was used by the ancient Egyptians in their mummification processes and amber has been moulded and used for ornaments and jewellery from at least the same period. Tortoiseshell, too, has been used in a decorative sense for centuries and papier maché flourished in the eighteenth century.

Horn has been used since ancient times either as drinking vessels or a signalling device. In sheet form it has been used for lanterns, knife handles, spoons, moulded boxes, and, again, in the eighteenth century as a substitute for glass. Horn is a natural plastic from the horns of various animals such as rams and goats, and is based on keratin. It was used for decorative goods such as medallions in the 1620s. By the beginning of the eighteenth century London was a major centre for horn, where makers such as John Obrisset produced a range of elaborately moulded snuff boxes.

The manufacture of combs was perhaps one of the most important applications of horn, particularly between 1770 and 1880. The horn comb-making industry became so important that centres were set up devoted to this trade, notably in La Val Plastiques, at Oyonnax in the Jura Mountains, France, and in Leominster, Massachusetts, America. Many of the techniques applied to manufacture horn combs, in terms of pressing into mouldings and cutting, were later applied to the plastics industry. Indeed Oyonnax later became the centre of the Celluloid comb industry in the late nineteenth and early twentieth centuries and is still a centre for designer-led plastics today. Interestingly enough jewellery forms that appeared to be horn were later copied in vulcanised rubber. Many techniques which were traditionally used to form objects of horn, such as pressing into flat sheets and moulding into simple shapes, were later adapted to shaping semi-synthetic plastics.

SHELLAC

Shellac is a natural plastic which combines the refined excretion of the lac beetle mixed with fillers. The insect is mainly found on certain trees in Burma, Thailand and India and has been harvested since ancient times. After mixing the lac beetle's excretion with a number of different fillers, such as wood flour and slate dust, the shellac was pressed into a heated mould, and when the mould had cooled the object was released.

Shellac was used in solidified form to make a range of goods such as decorative mirror backs and boxes. In North America Sam Peck patented the Union Case in 1854, prior to the American Civil War. Union cases consisted of a shellac, moulded box with an elaborately intricate surface. The case was designed to hold the two types of photograph of the day: daguerreotypes (polished and silvered copper plate) and ambrotypes (glass collodion positives). The Union Case contained these photographic equivalents of the

HORN IS
A NATURAL
PLASTIC
FROM THE
HORNS OF
VARIOUS
ANIMALS
SUCH AS
RAMS AND
GOATS, AND
IS BASED
ON KERATIN

IN MESOAMERICA AS
EARLY AS 1600 BC
THE MAYANS PLAYED A
PARTICULARLY BLOOD-
THIRSTY BALL GAME. THE
RULES WERE NOT TO LET
THE BALL TOUCH THE
FLOOR OF THE COURT.
THE UNFORTUNATES WHO
DROPPED THE BALL WERE
DECAPITATED AND HAD
THEIR HEADS WRAPPED IN
RUBBER AND THESE WERE
THEN USED AS THE BALLS
FOR THE REMAINDER OF
THE GAME

The raw seeds used to make rubber, each seed is usually approximately one inch in length.

owners' beloveds in a dark environment, a necessary precaution, as the early glass positives faded in light.

Shellac has excellent moulding capabilities and so could be cut with a rose lathe and also reproduced with a fine degree of detail. Usually Union cases were decorated with geometric patterns. Sometimes very skilled die engravers produced designs based on famous contemporary paintings, such as John Vanderlyn's *Landing of Columbus*. Over a thousand designs of Union case are known. In 1887, the superior moulding capability of shellac was exploited in the production of shellac records which took over from the wax cylinder. Shellac records continued to be produced until they were superseded by the vinyl copolymer record, Union Carbide's Vinylite, in 1948.

NATURAL RUBBER

Natural rubber was used in Mesoamerica as early as 1600 BC. Later, as recorded in the sacred Mayan text, the Popol Vuh, the Mayans played a particularly blood-thirsty ball game. The rules were not to let the ball touch the floor of the court. The unfortunates who dropped the ball were decapitated and had their heads wrapped in rubber and these were then used as the balls for the remainder of the game. By the time the Spanish Conquistadors, who invaded South America in the sixteenth century, witnessed this game in the 1550s they regarded it as simply an amusing entertainment! Perhaps there is a lesson in discipline to be learned for modern football matches and failures in penalty shoot-outs! The Peruvians used latex rubber to make cloaks and galoshes as well as ornamental goods, and it was from them that the Spanish Conquistadors learned how to coat their stockings, and then their boots and cloaks in latex rubber to make them comfortable and waterproof for life in the jungle.

Natural rubber (also known as latex or caoutchouc) is collected as sap from the *Hevea Brasiliensis* rubber tree, native to Brazil. The sap is immersed in acid to extract the water, producing a solid that can then be rolled into sheets, dried and cured. Refined extrusion, after the curing stage, replaces the water evacuation process, and following more processing, rubber is calendared into sheets, and then cut into shapes, compression-moulded or extruded. Natural rubber was first brought into Britain in 1792 by the French explorer and physicist, Charles Marie de La Condamine. Initially natural rubber was used by architects and draftsmen as erasers. However, it then became popular for waterproof cloaks and boots. Contemporary cartoons from around 1815 illustrate that this wonder material was being used in a variety of ways and was being actively promoted and advertised.

Unfortunately natural, unmodified, rubber becomes rigid in the cold and, conversely, becomes sticky and melts in heat, rendering it impractical. Charles Macintosh found that coal tar oil was a good solvent for rubber, producing a solution, India rubber, which, when coated between two fabrics, resulted in a very satisfactory waterproof fabric. Macintosh used this for double texture waterproofed cloaks known as Macintoshes, first produced in 1824, the first truly practical waterproof rubber garment.

In the nineteenth century, machinery was developed and improved to produce a variety of rubber goods. These included Thomas Hancock's masticator, which cut up rubber into smaller pieces using spiked rollers, producing a doughy, workable mass that could then be moulded.

RUBBER SUPPLY
Supplies of rubber were ensured when, in 1876, Sir Henry Wickham brought back 70,000 rubber seeds from Brazil, smuggled on a ship he chartered called the *Amazonas*. Wickham had been hired to do this by Dr Joseph Hooker, the Director of the Botanical Gardens at Kew, London. Only about 3.75 per cent of the seeds were successfully geminated and then used to set up rubber plantations in Malaysia (some were also sent to India and

Rubber was used to waterproof clothing by the Peruvians. Today waterproof workwear uses polyethene, polyurethane, flexothane, or rubber to protect the worker from the weather, damp and dirt. This allows work to be undertaken in a vast array of circumstances without discomfort.

Singapore). Wickham said he had been given the seeds, although it seems that he had openly collected them over a series of months in the Amazon area, despite later accusations of theft. However, the rubber seeds made many people's fortunes and opened a consumer market for a range of new rubber goods, not least the emerging tyre industry. Wickham himself was paid £700 and eventually gained a knighthood in 1920 for his work for the rubber industry, suggesting that although his life was beset by setbacks, and questionable practice, the rubber seed interlude stood him in good stead.

In 1928 a method for making foam from latex rubber was developed by the Dunlop Rubber Company, as was the Freeze-gel process, developed by the Talalay brothers. These have an important application in the Dunlopillo mattress, a synthetic mattress that made beds hygienic and non-allergic but also breathable due to the array of holes moulded into the foam. These foaming methods were later used with synthetic rubbers too.

THE RUBBER SEEDS MADE MANY PEOPLE'S FORTUNES AND OPENED A CONSUMER MARKET FOR A RANGE OF NEW RUBBER GOODS, NOT LEAST THE EMERGING TYRE INDUSTRY

GUTTA PERCHA

Gutta percha, a close relative of rubber, became popular in the mid-nineteenth century. It is a natural plastic made from an isomer of rubber exuded from the Palaquium tree, native to Malaysia. Dark brown in colour, it can be shaped by softening over heat and pressing into cold moulds. Alternatively it can be shaped by extrusion, ie. pushed through holes to produce tubes or other profiles. The *Gutta Percha* Company was set up in 1845 by Charles Hancock (the brother of Thomas Hancock) and Henry Bewley (famed for being the creator of the first rubber extruding machine). Bewley adapted equipment, already in use to extrude rubber, to produce *gutta percha* tubes. Hancock and Bewley later fell out, but their company produced a range of decorative goods which were illustrated in fancily designed, bound catalogues and were also displayed at the Great Exhibition of 1851 in London.

Wire insulated with *gutta percha* was laid across the Hudson River at Fort Lee in August, 1849, for the Morse Telegraph Company in America. *Gutta percha* possesses excellent insulating properties, in 1851, *gutta percha* tubes were used to cover the first submarine cable between France and England. The first transatlantic cable was successfully laid at the second attempt of Isambard Kingdom Brunel's Great Eastern steamship in 1866. Used to make golf balls which were nick named "gutties", *gutta percha* was utilised for a variety of other applications, including decorative mouldings, ear trumpets, cable insulation and dental fillings. However, sometimes its application outreached its functionality. An example of this is the *gutta percha* sideboard, displayed at the Great Exhibition of 1851, where the pendulous fruit which ornamented the sideboard fell off during the course of the exhibition. A contemporary account described *gutta percha* as "a treacherous material".

The rubber and *gutta percha* industries were not without a human cost. The local indigenous workers, who obtained the sap from the trees in South America and the Congo, which gave latex rubber and *gutta percha*, were exploited on the plantations and often suffered brutal punishments if they did not fulfil their quota. It was estimated that in the Congo at the end of the nineteenth century a rubber worker's life was worth ten kilograms of rubber. In South America, according to Sir Roger Casement's report of 1912, 4,000 tons of rubber cost the lives of at least 30,000 indigenous Indians.

OPPOSITE: *Gutta percha* items from the mid-1800s. By 1845, telegraph wires insulated with *gutta percha* were being manufactured in Britain. *Gutta percha* served as the insulating material for some of the earliest undersea telegraph cables, including the first transatlantic telegraph cable.

RIGHT: Charles Hancock, brother of Thomas Hancock, was a pioneer of *gutta percha*. Mid-nineteenth century.

In the mid-nineteenth century, *gutta percha* was also used to make furniture. Followers of the design reform movement, who also supported truth and honesty in materials, criticised this use.

IT WAS ESTIMATED THAT IN THE CONGO AT THE END OF THE NINETEENTH CENTURY A RUBBER WORKER'S LIFE WAS WORTH TEN KILOGRAMS OF RUBBER

John Loadman

BOIS DURCI

Bois Durci literally translates as "hard wood" and was invented by François Charles Lepage, who patented it in Britain in 1856. Mainly produced between 1855 and the late 1880s, it is a form of wood pulp moulding made from sawdust (from a hardwood such as ebony or rosewood) mixed with egg or blood albumen. The sawdust could be mixed with any vegetable, mineral or metallic powders and the albumen with any other glutinous or gelatinous substance. The powder was soaked in albumen diluted with water, dried and then compressed in a steel mould under steam, heat and pressure. *Bois Durci* is a natural plastic which was used to make decorative mouldings, most often in the form of plaques commemorating famous people such as Shakespeare and Napoleon. The plaques are frequently stamped with the trade name *Bois Durci* as well as the trademark of a feather which appears beneath the moulded head. *Bois Durci* was used to make inkwells and pen trays as well as ornamental plaques for furniture and doors.

Bois Durci is a natural plastic moulding material based on blood, egg albumen and sawdust. It was patented in Paris, in 1855, by Lepage. Some authorities state that *Bois Durci* went out of use by the late 1880s, but recent research shows that it was still being produced under the *Bois Durci* name even after the First World War.

OPPOSITE: *Bois Durci* plaque of Napoleon.

TOP AND BOTTOM: Two *Bois Durci* encrier (ink-wells).

All images courtesy of Harold Mernick.

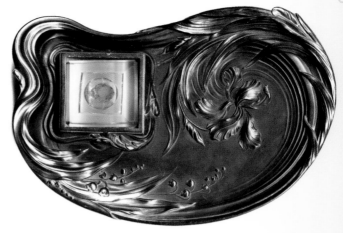

SEMI-SYNTHETIC PLASTICS AND THE NINETEENTH CENTURY

Mourning or memorial jewellery has been worn since the Middle Ages and became popular in the fifteenth and sixteenth century in Britain. Until the eighteenth century it generally consisted of gold and black enamel, often in the form of a skull. From 1770, forms became lighter and more graceful, often incorporating hair in their designs and in the early eighteenth century fine scrolled rings were made.

In the nineteenth century, with the demise of Prince Albert in 1861, mourning dress was worn by a widow for a year and a day, followed by nine months of half mourning, where black was not a necessity but sombre colours were advised.

Favourite symbols used in mourning jewellery included flowers, hearts, crosses, and ivy leaves, which replaced the earlier more macabre symbols of skulls, coffins, and gravestones. Many memorial pieces bear the inscription "in memory of". Jet jewellery made from fossilised wood was an acceptable commodity often worn for mourning, and coral and pearls were allowed at court as half mourning jewellery.

Semi-synthetic plastics came to the fore in the mid-nineteenth century—a period of great experimentation in materials in Britain and America. This was the time when rubber was first vulcanised (made hard) by adding sulphur. The English inventor, Thomas Hancock, who took credit for this discovery, had previously developed a method of cutting up rubber in his 'masticator', creating fragments that could then be reformed into a new product. Up to this point it had not been possible to rework or reuse rubber once it had been formed.

VULCANITE

Although Thomas Hancock patented the vulcanisation of rubber first in 1843, it seems that he may have borrowed the idea from Charles Goodyear, an American, who submitted his patent in 1844. Hancock's friend, Henry Brockeden, brought a piece of hardened rubber, which he had obtained from Goodyear, and showed it to Hancock, who then developed his vulcanised rubber using his 'vulcaniser'. Charles Goodyear himself may even have been inspired by another American, Nathaniel Hayward, to develop his hardened rubber. Whatever the truth, Goodyear was to die in poverty, following a life in and out of debtor's prison, whereas Hancock went on to great fortune. Hancock combined his skills for invention with entrepreneurship and self-publicity to make a name for himself in the early semi-synthetic plastics industry. He even made a plaque of himself in his vulcanised rubber. Hancock published his invention widely in catalogues and in his memoir, *A History of Caoutchouc*, he writes of his personal discovery of vulcanised rubber. An annotated copy of this book, once owned by his British contemporary, Alexander Parkes, reveals that Parkes thought "this discovery was first made by Goodyear... and not by Hancock". However, in Hancock's defence, those who worked with him admired his work ethic and process, and were loyal, long-serving associates. Hancock called his substance "Vulcanite" after the Roman god, Vulcan who, in mythology, worked with heat and sulphur.

Vulcanite became popular as mourning jewellery, after the death of Prince Albert in 1861, because of its ability to imitate jet.[1] Vulcanite is a semi-synthetic plastic and is made of rubber hardened with sulphur, known as Ebonite or Hard Rubber in America. The material is the first truly semi-synthetic plastic, as it is made from a natural material, rubber, which has been chemically altered—the rubber's composition and properties being changed by the addition of sulphur under controlled conditions. Vulcanite was popular for items such as pens and Vesta match boxes, goods which were often designed to commemorate an event, such as Queen Victoria's Jubilee, and were an early form of mass-produced memorabilia aimed at a specific market. The material is characteristically black in colour, but when mixed with

VULCANITE WAS THE FIRST TRULY SEMI-SYNTHETIC PLASTIC

white and red pigments produced a pink substance which could be made to resemble gums for false dentures. One of its widespread uses today is for tyres. This use first began with the application of vulcanised rubber to the Robert William Thompson pneumatic tyre in June 1846. This was reinvented by John Boyd Dunlop in 1888. Tyres became increasingly important as the century progressed with the development of the automobile which came into its own in the 1890s. By this time Vulcanite was also to play an important role, as insulation for both the cables and the early plugs and sockets used in the emerging electrical industry.

EXHIBITING PLASTIC

Experimentation in new materials and products was spurred on by public events, such as the Great Exhibition of 1851 and the International Exhibition of 1862 held in Hyde Park, London. The first exhibition was organised by the Prince Consort, Prince Albert, and others, including Sir Henry Cole, to celebrate modern industrial technology and design. Attracting six million visitors, this exhibition showcased the consumer goods available, and was accompanied by lavishly illustrated catalogues of the exhibits.

EXPERIMENTATION IN NEW MATERIALS AND PRODUCTS WAS SPURRED ON BY PUBLIC EVENTS

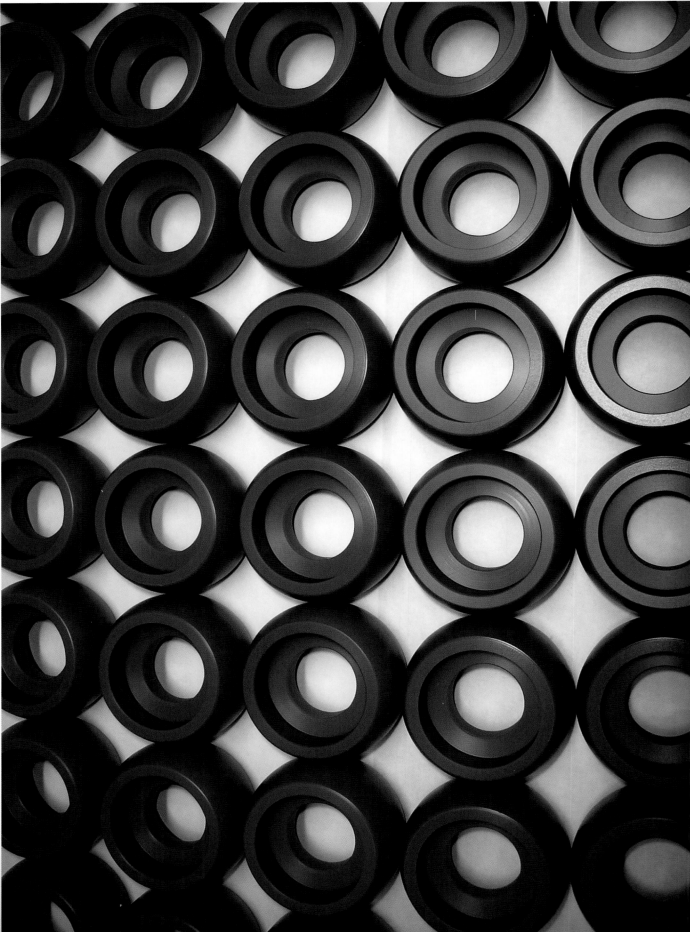

62

PARKESINE

The semi-synthetic plastic, Parkesine—based on cellulose nitrate, also known as pyroxyline—was displayed in 1862 at the International Exhibition in Hyde Park, where it won a bronze medal for excellence of product and a silver medal at the Paris Universal Exhibition in 1867. This plastic was made from a mixture of cotton fibres or cotton flock and nitric acid and was the forerunner of the commercially successful Celluloid. Following his exhibition success, Parkes then set up the Parkesine Company in 1866, financed by a range of friends and colleagues, notably Sir Henry Bessemer of Bessemer steel fame. The Parkesine factory was located in Hackney Wick, East London.

Parkes was an assiduous inventor, with 66 patents to his name, mainly related to metallurgy, but also including ones concerned with India rubber, and *gutta percha* as well as Parkesine. His patent for vulcanising rubber was bought for £5,000 by Thomas Hancock. Unfortunately Parkes failed in making a successful business of Parkesine—possibly due to his obsession with producing his material for a shilling a pound. This meant that he may have used inferior materials or allowed his product insufficient curing time. He received complaints that his combs were wrinkled and quite useless.

Rather than being a trained chemist, Parkes was originally educated as an artisan craftsman and was a skilled artist and sculptor. The drawings in his notebooks reveal a high degree of artistic skill and the records tell us that he had sufficient expertise to produce a worthy copy of a Reuben's cartoon on a house wall near his home. He was to apply his artistic skills to designing a range of decorative goods including hair slides inlaid with silver and brass as well as decorative medallions and plaques with pictorial scenes, and even a miniature head of Jesus Christ. Throughout his life, he was heavily dependent on his brother, Henry Parkes, who had trained at the Royal Chemical College, and Alexander Parkes presumably relied on Henry for the rigorous scientific input into his inventions and patents.

However, the Parkesine Company failed and went into liquidation in 1868. Parkes' works manager, Daniel Spill, was to eventually take over Parkes patents much to Parkes' displeasure as he had not got on very well with Spill. Spill renamed the material Ivoride and Xylonite (for the coloured version) and set up his Xylonite Company. He made a range of spectacular and rather ill-founded claims for his material. The 1869 Xylonite Company price list calls Xylonite: "An excellent substitute for ivory, bone, tortoiseshell, Horn, Hard Woods, Vulcanite etc.—it is not at all affected by chemicals or atmospheric changes, and therefore valuable for shipment to hot climates." Spill produced the handles of knives and forks as well as a range of decorative goods such as mirrors and imitation coral brooches. He appears to have had a strong role in the design of his goods as he was a

OPPOSITE: Objects made from Parkesine, 1855-1868. The items include a decorative plate, a medallion, hair slides, experimental pieces, two trademarked discs, ornaments, a snuff box and a decorative plaque. Parkesine is thought to have been the first semi-synthetic plastic, a mouldable cellulose nitrate which was invented by Alexander Parkes (1813-1890). It was made of cotton fibres dissolved in nitric and sulphuric acids and mixed with vegetable oil. It was softened by heat and then moulded or hand-carved. Parkesine's great disadvantage, however, was its high flammability. Although Parkes took out a number of patents for his newly discovered material in the 1860s, it was not until the Hyatt brothers of New Jersey developed it as Celluloid that its commercial potential began to be realised. Image courtesy of Science and Society.

OPPOSITE: Xylonite and
Ivoride objects, circa 1862,
manufactured by Daniel Spill.
The handles of the two knives
and the delicate hair comb
is made of Ivoride. The red
jewellery is part of a set
imitating coral. Pictured here is
a necklace and a cravat pin with
a red xylonite head. The small
hand mirror and death's head
handle (and Spill's own), are
both made from Ivoride. Ivoride
and xylonite are made
of cellulose nitrate in a form
based on that developed by
Alexander Parkes. Image
courtesy of Science and Society.

strong draftsman, and drawings exist of his design for his Ivoride mirror back.

Spill's business was also to fail and he assigned Parkes' associated patents to the British Xylonite Company. This company was able to manufacture Xylonite successfully at Hale End. Their trademark was an elephant and tortoise standing side by side. Perhaps a reflection on the idea that their imitation ivory and tortoiseshell Xylonite products were saving the elephant and tortoise from extinction. However, the late nineteenth century was an unexpectedly early date for environmental awareness.

An off-shoot of the cellulose nitrate industry was the first artificial silk. Called Chardonnet silk after its French inventor, Count Hilaire de Chardonnet, it was patented in 1884 and caused a sensation when it was exhibited at the Paris Exhibition of 1889 where it was awarded the Grand Prix. Unfortunately its highly flammable nature caused its downfall, due to the contemporary fashion for voluminous dresses and candlelight. Needless to say, dresses made of Chardonnet silk caught fire and the material was banned in France, becoming known as widow's silk. Undeterred, de Chardonnet set up a factory at Wolston near Coventry and produced Wolston silk. Surprisingly, the Wolston silk was again based on cellulose nitrate and equally as flammable.

DRESSES MADE OF CHARDONNET SILK CAUGHT FIRE AND THE MATERIAL WAS BANNED IN FRANCE, BECOMING KNOWN AS WIDOW'S SILK

CELLULOID

It was in America that the real success story developed with Celluloid mouldable material based on cellulose nitrate, developed by the brothers John Wesley and Isaiah Hyatt. The pair's initial aim was to find a suitable material to replace the ivory for billiard balls, as tusks became more rare and therefore expensive. A $10,000 prize was offered by the New York firm, Phelan & Collender, for a substitute material for ivory, to be made into the balls. The Hyatts learned of Alexander Parkes' work on a mouldable compound based on cellulose nitrate (called pyroxyline)—John Hyatt acknowledging this in a speech he gave in 1914, when he was awarded the prestigious American Perkin medal.[2] As early as December 1865, in a paper given to the Royal Society of Arts, Parkes had stated that Parkesine was a suitable replacement for ivory and tortoiseshell. Initially the Hyatt brothers set up the Albany Billiard Ball Company in 1870, to manufacture cellulose nitrate material. Their material was not without its problems, especially concerning flammability. There is an account of how their new billiard balls exploded during a billiards game in a saloon in Colorado, and everyone present drew their gun, assuming a fight had broken out.

By 1872, the Hyatt brothers had settled on the name Celluloid for their material, and set up the Celluloid Company. John Hyatt was not only a practical inventor but also possessed good business skills, and the pair identified a gap in the consumer market, designing their goods specifically to fit into it. The Hyatt brothers managed to make a commercial success of Celluloid by working closely with engineer, Charles Burroughs, to develop reliable methods and machines for manufacture, and also by using camphor, a strong-smelling compound, as a plasticiser and solvent.[3] Alexander Parkes had also previously used camphor, but had also worked with a range of other materials. In 1881 he commented that Parkesine and Celluloid plastics were all the same (due to their camphor content).

In addition to making Celluloid combs, the Hyatts also made Celluloid collars and cuffs. This meant that the humble working-class man, who could not afford to have his linen laundered on a daily basis, had access to a cheap solution—a wipe-clean collar and cuffs. This perhaps was a democratising step for the working man whose status was synonymous with the collarless shirt. Unfortunately, if a heavy drinker wore such a Celluloid collar, this secret would be revealed as the collar turned pink, discoloured by the drinker's sweat.

Flammability caused a problem when cigar smokers wore Celluloid dentures—these are known to have gone up in flames, a risk inherent with such a flammable material. Elaborate decorative Celluloid combs were made

Objects made from Celluloid, 1920s–1930s. Celluloid, like Parkesine, is based on cellulose nitrate but includes camphor as a plasticiser, making moulding easier. It was patented in America in 1870. Early applications included billiard balls, knife handles and small decorative items, often successfully imitating ivory or tortoiseshell. Once it was cast as film, Celluloid made the development of cinema possible. Image courtesy of Science and Society.

NEW BILLIARD BALLS EXPLODED DURING A BILLIARDS GAME IN A SALOON IN COLORADO, AND EVERYONE PRESENT DREW THEIR GUN, ASSUMING A FIGHT HAD BROKEN OUT

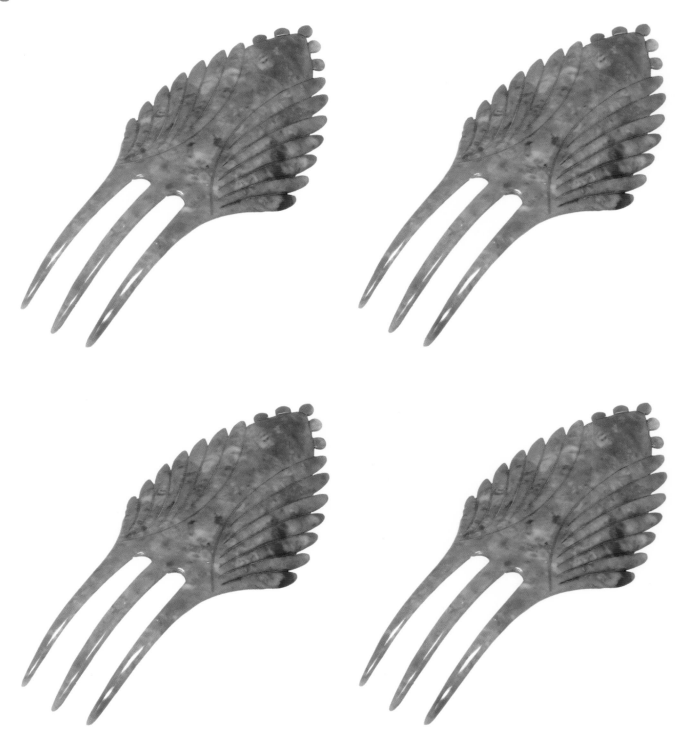

by French designers such as Auguste Bonaz and Clement Joyard but Celluloid
sheet had more practical applications in semi-transparent form—utilised in
goggles and car windows. The latter were known to crack, craze, degrade and
fail and would be replaced by whatever was to hand.[4] In one extraordinary
case, dating to the 1940s, side windows were replaced by recycled chest
x-rays supplied by the car driver's matron sister! Celluloid was also used for
toothbrushes handles and combs but fell rapidly in popularity in the 1920s,
with the coming of the short bobbed hairstyle and, literally, a much smaller
market for hair products. Now largely fallen into disuse, Celluloid is still used
to make components of mortar bombs, for the pearlised veneer finishes of
popstars' drum kits and also in ping-pong balls.

Celluloid was to play a vital role in the development of film—a fact that is
universally understood. As early as 1856, Parkes took out a provisional patent
for substituting his new material, Parkesine, for the heavy glass negative
plates currently in use in the film industry. In 1870, Spill lectured to the
London Photographic Society and mentioned that he hoped that he would one
day, from Xylonite, be able to produce, "a flexible and structureless substitute
for the glass negative supports". Parkes even produced some thin Parkesine
(cellulose nitrate) films in the 1850s. However, this concept was way ahead
of its time and it was the Hyatt brothers who made the next leap, with the
development of a Celluloid film thin enough to take photographic negatives.
The Hyatts worked with George Eastman, of Eastman Kodak fame, to produce
a thin Celluloid film and, by 1885, a satisfactory thin film medium had been
developed. This led to the birth of the Celluloid industry that we now know
as Hollywood, although Celluloid film was very flammable and was eventually
replaced by cellulose acetate safety film in 1948.

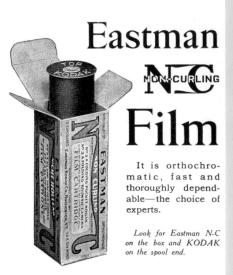

Full Kodak efficiency is
realized only in the use of

Eastman
N-C NON-CURLING

Film

It is orthochro-
matic, fast and
thoroughly depend-
able—the choice of
experts.

*Look for Eastman N-C
on the box and KODAK
on the spool end.*

EASTMAN KODAK CO.
ROCHESTER, N. Y.

CELLULOSE ACETATE

In 1865, Paul Schützenberger was the first person to prepare cellulose acetate, heating cotton with acetic anhydride in closed tubes at 130–140C (around 280F). Techniques were gradually refined for controlling acetylation under less severe conditions. By 1910 the Dreyfus brothers (Henri and Camille) had made cellulose acetate photographic film. Cellulose acetate had been produced as a non-flammable form of cellulose nitrate, although it was often perceived by those in the business as not such an attractive material. The Dreyfus brothers built a factory at Spondon, Derbyshire at the outbreak of the First World War to produce cellulose acetate (diacetate) dissolved in acetone, commonly referred to as "dope", and used to coat the fabric wings of aircraft. It replaced the dangerously flammable cellulose nitrate lacquers. By the end of the war there was a glut of cellulose acetate, and Dr Henry Dreyfus researched ways of turning this surplus material into a new product, Celanese fibres. The superfluity of cellulose acetate led to the production, in 1918, of cellulose acetate rod, sheet and household products such as lampshades.

Due to its lack of flammability, cellulose acetate was used, in preference to cellulose nitrate, as a substitute for glass, in car window's interlayers and goggles. Cellulose acetate was not made in a mouldable powder form until 1929, when it was soon produced using the injection moulding process developed by Dr Arthur Eichengrün. It was one of the only plastics which was injection-moulded until after the Second World War, although injection moulding is now the most common process used to shape plastics. In 1931, cellulose acetate was used for the 80 metre high, Helicoidal Tower, at the Paris International Exhibition and later still, utility buckles and toys were made from the malleable material.

RAYON

In 1892, Charles Cross and Edward Bevan discovered a way of turning cellulose acetate into artificial fibres. Initially the fibres took the form of cellulose xanthate, and later as regenerated cellulose acetate, made from cotton fibres treated with caustic soda. Cross and Bevan discovered that it was possible to make fibres from this material, producing a viscous liquid which could then be spun into fibres. Cross called this invention viscose and they made a variety of both fibres and solid goods, such as umbrella handles, from this material. They sold their patents to

1. Jet is a geological material derived from decaying wood under extreme pressure. The substance is either black or dark brown and the adjective jet-black is better-known, perhaps, than the substance from which the descriptive phrase derives.

2. The Perkin Medal was established to commemorate the 50th anniversary of the discovery of mauvene. Today it is now widely acknowledged as the highest honour in American industrial chemistry. Perkin was a founding Member of SCI and this Medal was first presented in New York to Perkin himself.

3. Camphor is also used in medicinal creams for its mild antiseptic and anti-itching properties and, as an aside to plastics, is also utilised in explosives.

4. A series of or the forming of very fine cracks in the surface of a material, usually a polymeric substance. Crazing is generally caused by chemical attack or other degrading agents such as ultraviolet radiation.

Courtaulds in 1904, who then went on to rename the product viscose Rayon, achieving worldwide success. Rayon was attractive and could be made in a variety of weights and finishes to imitate natural fabrics such as gauze, silk and brocades. Those who made Rayon knew how to sell it; one man being so excited by this material that he dedicated his book, *The Romance of Rayon*, to the plastic. Courtaulds mounted an active advertising campaign which glamorised their product. Viscose Rayon, made artificial silk affordable, especially to those on lower incomes. The story was told to Percy Reboul of the Plastics Historical Society, of a girl working in the British Xylonite factory. She was stationed in the acid house of the factory and wearing a Rayon dress. Luckily the dress was not flammable, but was so badly damaged by the acid that she left work with a dress full of holes.

Cellulose acetate in fibre form underwent another modification in the late twentieth century. Products, such as Tencel and Lyocell fibres, have been made using cellulose acetate, which applied more sustainable and environmentally friendly manufacturing methods, with water used as a solvent rather than acid. One person who seized on cellulose acetate as a moulding material was Eduard Fornells Marco, an Andorran craftsman who worked in the ateliers of René Lalique in Paris. He designed a cellulose acetate box decorated with cherries, an item which has now become a collector's piece. He then established his own workshops in Paris and produced a range of goods under the trade name Editions Fornells, which focused on decorative boxes. He made the same form in cellulose acetate and later used urea formaldehyde; he produced his own version of the synthetic billiard ball in a material based on urea formaldehyde which he called Formatch.

Cellulose acetate was also used for more practical applications such as keys on calculating machines and typewriter, as well as for spectacle frames. It also became a popular material for packaging. As Cellophane, invented in 1908, it reached a wider market and is still in use today and has been immortalised in the musical, *Chicago*, in the song, Mr Cellophane.

RAYON WAS ATTRACTIVE AND COULD BE MADE IN A VARIETY OF WEIGHTS AND FINISHES TO IMITATE NATURAL FABRICS SUCH AS GAUZE, SILK AND BROCADES

CASEIN

By the late nineteenth century, casein (casein-formaldehyde) was developed—a milk-based semi-synthetic plastic. Patented in 1899, in Germany, by Adolphe Spittler under the trade name Galalith, in Britain it was called Syrolit (1909) and later Erinoid (1914). It also had the trade names Lactoid and Ikilith. Casein material could be produced in a variety of 'pure' colours, from imitation horn and tortoiseshell, to a variety of pearlised colours—the addition of fish scales gave this pearl effect. A particularly popular use of casein was in buttons, but as casein distorts in the damp, it has been largely replaced in buttons by machine-washable plastics such as polyesters and acrylics. Casein was made into pen barrels and desk equipment, knitting needles, decorative goods and stylish Art Deco jewellery. Casein was applied as a veneer on furniture and gramophones. Austrian designer, Josef Olbrich, applied casein to a clock, dated to 1902. The Scottish designer, Charles Rennie Mackintosh, applied casein to furniture and clocks at least as early as 1919.

OPPOSITE: Grinding machinery used to produce casein plastic, 1900. The intricate machine was used at BP Chemicals, Stroud, Gloucestershire. The machinery was manufactured by Bauermeister Ottensen. Image courtesy Science and Society.

BOTTOM: Display card of Erinoid plastic, circa 1930. These samples were for use in door handles and are made of casein, produced by Erinoid Limited. Casein is a semi-synthetic plastic present in skimmed milk. A rennet is used to precipitate it out. The casein is mixed with water, dyes or pigments and drawn out into shapes for machining. It is then cured by immersing it into a solution of formaldehyde. The plastic is then suitable for use in making furniture handles, buttons and other decorative items. Erinoid was the British trade name for casein formaldehyde in the 1920s and 1930s. Image courtesy Science and Society.

SYNTHETIC PLASTICS AND THE TWENTIETH CENTURY

OPPOSITE: Bakelite face phantom for practising eye operations, made by Leiter of Vienna, Austria. Image courtesy of Science and Society.

BOTTOM: The second Pouva Start Camera 1956. Resulting from Karl Pouva's successful camera factory in Freital near Dresden, the Pouva camera became an affordable alternative product suitable as a beginner's camera. This second Pouva Start model has an enhanced appearance, as well as extra features, including an optical finder.

It took the work of a brilliant chemist and successful businessman, Leo Baekeland to make the first synthetic plastic, Bakelite, a worldwide success story. The inventor of Bakelite, Leo Baekeland was a self-made man, born into poverty in Ghent, in 1863. Baekeland was the son of a cobbler and sometime inn-keeper and a mother who was a domestic servant who had seen how the wealthy lived and was keen for her son to better himself. Baekeland was to achieve greatness both due to his mother's encouragement and his own considerable efforts and talents.

EARLY DEVELOPMENT

Awarded his doctorate by the age of 21, Baekeland was an assistant professor by the time he made his first trip to the US, in 1889, on a travelling scholarship, after his marriage to his professor's daughter, the beautiful Céline Swarts. He was never to make his home in Belgium again, and gave up his academic university post to go into work for A & HT Anthony & Company. During his early days in America, money was tight, so much so that he used the silver from his watch chain, a gift from his father, as raw material for some of his early experiments—perhaps as much a reflection on his lack of affection for his father as for his poverty. Baekeland had sent his wife back to Belgium for the

UNLESS I AM VERY MUCH MISTAKEN, THIS INVENTION WILL PROVE IMPORTANT IN THE FUTURE

Leo Baekeland's diary, 11 July, 1907

OPPOSITE: Bakelite advertising touting it as 'The Material of a Thousand Uses', December, 1923.

birth of their first child and did not send for her again for over a year—a rift from which their marriage never recovered. Baekeland then suffered a ruptured appendix, which, despite almost killing him, focused his mind, convincing him that he should concentrate on a single goal. He later commented that "sometimes it is an advantage for a man of genius not to know too much" as "too much book knowledge" might "petrify the mind".

KODAK

Baekeland developed Velox photographic paper which he sold for $750,000 in 1899 to Eastman Kodak, via some clever negotiation. This was a fortune that made Baekeland independently wealthy and therefore able to choose what he wanted to work on. He also learned a vital business lesson: it was important to give clear instructions for the use of a product, as those who already knew the business would not even read the instructions. This type of behaviour was to cause some users of his Velox paper to use it in the wrong way and gain poor results. Baekeland was to find the same sort of practice evident in his initial days of working with established moulding companies, to manufacture Bakelite. He had to constantly supervise the work, correcting major mistakes.

Baekeland decided to focus his research on phenolic resins as his aim was to find a substitute for shellac which was heavily in use as a lacquer at the time.

Developed in 1907, Bakelite was the result of five years dedicated research. Leo Baekeland had built a laboratory next to his home at Yonkers, New York. Here he was able to carry out his work, helped by his assistant Nathaniel Thurlow, experimenting with two chemicals—formaldehyde and phenol. It was only when he combined them at over 150C (around 300F), under pressure and with an alkaline catalyst that his dream became a reality.

Baekeland was not the only person working in the field of phenolic resins at the time and his most challenging competitor was a Scotsman, Sir James Swinburne, whom he fortunately beat to the patent office by one day with his own patent for phenolic resins. On 15 July 1907, Baekeland wrote: "I have an excellent thing and it would be a great disappointment if my patent had been preceded by an earlier invention of somebody else."

SOMETIMES IT IS AN ADVANTAGE FOR A MAN OF GENIUS NOT TO KNOW TOO MUCH AS TOO MUCH BOOK KNOWLEDGE MIGHT PETRIFY THE MIND

Leo Baekeland

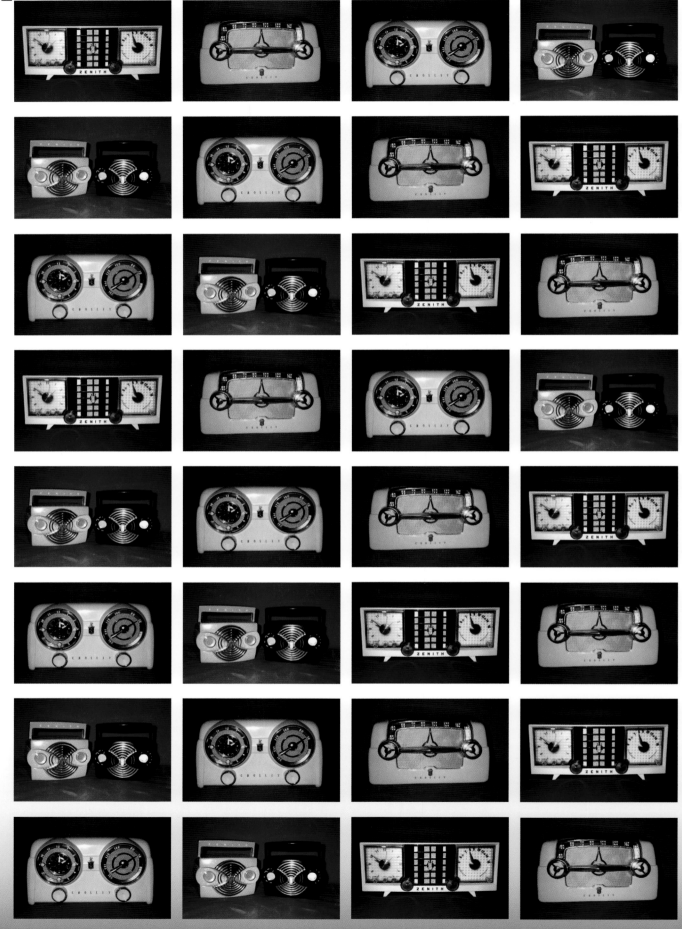

OPPOSITE: A selection of plastic radios, post-1945. From top left, Zenith radio in Bakelite; Crosley radio in aqua plastic; Crosley radio in green; Zenith radios in aqua and black plastic. These reflect the range of plastics available by 1945 and used in American radios. They might be seen as the antithesis of the 'good design' movement.

Baekeland managed to make his invention commercially viable by controlling the heat and pressure of the phenol formaldehyde reaction. In this he was aided by his 'Bakelizer'—a giant autoclave which he installed in his laboratory. Operating the Bakelizer became something of an event to which all Baekeland's family were invited. However, when the machine malfunctioned, the reaction could be dangerous and the Bakelizer was moved out of the laboratory after a particularly violent explosion.

Baekeland threw his energies into improving and promoting his new material, showing it to the visitors who came to his home. In October 1909, Baekeland made a triumphant presentation to the American Chemical Society about his new material and machine. He had taken time to produce perfect samples to showcase his material at its best and, in 1916, like John Wesley Hyatt before him, Baekeland was awarded the prestigious American Perkin medal.

By the time he invented Bakelite, Baekeland was already a wealthy man. A Belgian *émigré* who took American citizenship, he was the rare combination of a brilliant academic chemist combined with excellent business skills, who brought this focus into his Bakelite business. As a perfectionist, Baekeland was not satisfied with the way that the already-established companies were manufacturing his new Bakelite material, and by 1910 felt obliged to set up his own business: The General Bakelite Company. He remained director of the company, taking close interest in all of its affairs, until he sold the business to Union Carbide in 1939.

Early on in his career, Baekeland had envisaged a multiplicity of uses for his material, and by 1924 he had appeared on the front cover of *Time* magazine. In the accompanying article Baekeland was quoted saying, "This material has uses." The exposure that the article achieved meant that Baekeland, and his pioneering plastic, Bakelite, had finally achieved world renown.

GOOD DESIGN

Baekeland was persuaded by Allan Brown, who became Bakelite's public relations director in 1924, that good design was vital to the commercial success of the product. Brown organised a series of countrywide events focussing on the specifics of design, and hired the foremost designers of the day to work on Bakelite products. The results were instant design classics, such as the Bakelite Purma special camera for Thomas de la Rue. Brown also launched an advertising campaign where these designers gave a statement about the importance of good design and their opinion on the many facets of Bakelite. These adverts displayed flattering pictures of the designers as well as their products. This led to a series of well-designed Bakelite products which were streamlined, cutting edge and still recognised as design classics today.

THE MATERIAL OF A THOUSAND USES

In Britain, good design also became an important element in the success of the Ekco Radio Company Ltd, established by EK Cole in Southend. Cole employed key designers of the time to design casings for his range of radios, including the design luminaries Wells Wintemunte Coates, Serge Chermaeyeff, and Misha Black. These designers were architecturally trained and produced Bakelite radio casings in dark brown Bakelite that were architectural in form. Notable in the plethora of Bakelite products is the 1935, Wells Coates-designed, Ekco radio, AD36, which became a collectable design classic.

However, the British were rather more resistant to using plastics in the home. Bakelite domestic items and furniture was made in dark brown Bakelite, using fillers such as wood chips, so that products imitated wood or ebony. Indeed, after a period Ekco began making their radio casings of wood again for the British market. In America the public were far more receptive to good design and to Bakelite and a competition was organised to find an exceptional design for an all-Bakelite phone. American designer Henry Dreyfuss did not enter the competition but afterwards designed the Bakelite handset telephone which was manufactured for the Bell telephone company in 1937. This became another design classic which has endured until today and has been repeatedly replicated. In Britain the Siemens Neophone, made of Bakelite, had been produced in 1929, and was highly influential in terms of telephone design throughout the 1930s.

Baekeland had been assiduous in defending his numerous phenolic resin patents and vigorously sued those who infringed them. After a successful court battle against Redmanol and Condensite he then merged formally with them in 1923, forming the Bakelite Corporation.

In Britain, Baekeland's main competitor was the Damard Lacquer Company, run by Sir James Swinburne. With agreement from Baekeland, this company had taken over one of Baekeland's German-run subsidiaries, Bakelite Gesellshaft in Britain at the outbreak of the First World War. Swinburne had been astonished at how far in advance of his own company's manufacturing capabilities Bakelite Gesellshaft was. In 1928 Baekeland merged with the Damard Laquer Company in Britain, to form Bakelite Ltd.

Once Baekeland's patents ran out in 1928, it was possible for other companies to produce a range of new goods using phenolic resins. One of the notable companies who produced exciting new goods was the American Catalin Company, which produced a range of goods using cast phenolics. These did not need a filler and could be used to make a range of goods which imitated jade and amber, amongst other colours. Products made included decorative dressing table boxes designed on Art Deco principles and the classic cast phenolic FADA radio. America embraced this new range of colourful goods enthusiastically, and the Catalin Company used advertising as a tool to successfully emphasise the glamour of their new product.

THE BAKELITE HANDSET TELEPHONE BECAME ANOTHER DESIGN CLASSIC WHICH HAS ENDURED UNTIL TODAY

FORMICA

Formica is the trade name for a range of decorative laminates used for veneers for furniture, surfaces, soda fountains counters and even cruise liner interiors. The first phenolic sheet laminate was made of paper with a phenolic varnish, and, having been developed by Dan O'Connor around 1912, was patented in 1918. The Formica Insulation Company was formed in 1913 and, by the early 1920s, phenolic laminated sheets were used for radio casings. In the 1920s and 30s laminates were made using cloth or paper impregnated with phenol formaldehyde resins, and were dark coloured. The Formica Company introduced papers printed with wood grain designs. New colours and designs became possible in 1931 with the introduction of thiourea urea formaldehyde, urea and finally melamine coloured materials, in 1938. A sheet of patterned paper was impregnated with one of these materials and laminated under pressure onto underlayers impregnated with phenolic resin. The development of these laminates led to easy-care surfaces, particularly in the kitchen. To reduce cigarette damage, a foil underlayer was devised by John Cochrane Junior of the Formica Insulation Company.

Colorcore—a solid colour laminate built up from layers of coloured paper—was launched in 1983. Initially it was used in architectural and interior finishings and on furniture, then later in jewellery. Colorcore has been used by designers such as Frank Gehry and eminent British jewellery maker, Wendy Ramshaw.

Formica is a brand of composite materials manufactured by the Formica Corporation. In common use, the term refers to the company's classic product, a heat resistant, wipe-clean, plastic laminate of paper or fabric with melamine resin. The plastic was originally conceived as an electrical insulator, as a substitute for micarta, hence the similarity in name. Formica being an abbreviation of 'formerly micarta'. In its early years, Formica manufactured insulation along with other products such as phenolic composite gears, developing its classic range of surfacing laminates from the late 1920s. During the Second World War it manufactured plastic-impregnated wooden airplane propellers. Post-war, engineering uses declined, ceasing in 1970 in favour of decorative laminates.

OPPOSITE: Formica kitchen, circa 1955. A woman rinses vegetables in a wood-effect laminated kitchen. Photograph by Hulton Archive. Courtesy of Getty Images.

RIGHT: Colorcore assorted jewellery made by British designer, Wendy Ramshaw in the 1980s. Image courtesy of Wendy Ramshaw.

THE FORMICA COMPANY INTRODUCED PAPERS PRINTED WITH WOOD GRAIN DESIGNS

TOWARDS
COLOUR

Thiourea urea formaldehyde was developed in 1924 by Edmund Rossiter, who was working at the British Cyanides Company. This was a thermosetting plastic which could be produced in light, bright colours. Its early uses included being made into a range of attractive crockery in various colours, under trade names, such as Bandalasta and Beatl (later renamed Beetle). The plastic itself could be mixed with various pigments in powder form to produce a range of attractive goods. These were showcased by the London Department store, Harrods, which put on a display of multi-coloured Beetle and Bandalasta products in 1926. Bandalasta created a sensation with its appearance of fine, translucent porcelain.

UREA FORMALDEHYDE

Urea formaldehyde improved on thiourea formaldehyde. Developed by 1929, urea formaldehyde was marketed for a range of attractive uses. One area where it competed directly with Bakelite was in light, bright telephone handsets and for plugs and sockets. It was also used, in laminated form, to grace the boudoir scenes of many a Hollywood film set—with Ginger Rogers speaking on her white, new, ultra-feminine, urea formaldehyde phone. Previously white telephones had simply been made of black Bakelite which had been painted white. Urea formaldehydes brought more colour, combined with better properties, to the world of plastics. They were used for decorative applications and handbags, as well as more practical applications like light fittings. The light, bright colours of urea formaldehyde had a huge impact on design and the company, British Cyanides, produced 40 shades of cream and white alone.

In 1933, the Science Museum, London, held The Plastics Industry Exhibition, which proved so popular that its closing date was twice delayed. Within the exhibition was a room, the walls of which were covered with black phenolic laminates and orange urea formaldehyde laminates under the trade name Grenolin. Before polystyrene and polythene were invented, urea formaldehyde was the only synthetic plastic that could be made into brightly coloured, and relatively cheap, electrical mouldings, and colourful phones, lampshades and light fittings became must-have items for the home. In 1941, the nine-year-old future British actress, Diana Dors commented: "I am going to be a film star, with a swimming pool, and a cream telephone", epitomising the period's aspirational ideals.

UREA FORMALDEHYDES BROUGHT MORE COLOUR, COMBINED WITH BETTER PROPERTIES, TO THE WORLD OF PLASTICS

BELOW: Melamine powder.

OPPOSITE: Cabaret dancer
Lionel Blair testing the durability
of Melamine, a furniture surface
showcased at the 1960 Earls
Court Furniture Exhibition.
Photograph by Keystone.
Courtesy of Getty Images.

MELAMINE

Melamine resin was discovered by the German chemist, Baron
Justus von Liebig, in 1834, but the melamine formaldehyde
polymer was not patented until 1935, after which it was produced
commercially by the American Cyanamid Company, in 1939.
Melamine formaldehyde was water resistant and tougher than
urea formaldehyde and transparent, so that it became possible to
impregnate patterned papers for surfacing decorative laminates,
such as Formica and Warerite.

Melamine
99.8%min

Unison (Tianjin) Int'l Trading Co., Ltd.

MELAMINE FORMALDEHYDE WAS WATER RESISTANT AND TOUGHER THAN UREA FORMALDEHYDE

THE
PLASTICS
EXPLOSION

The 1930s saw a whole range of new plastics enter the scene. One of the earliest was the American synthetic rubber, neoprene. Originally called duprene, neoprene was the first mass-produced synthetic rubber compound. Neoprene's development was inspired by Father Julius Nieuwland, of the University of Notre Dame, located in Indiana, USA. Nieuwland was working on synthesising chloroprene from acetylene. The molecular structure of chloroprene is the same as isoprene (the building block of natural rubber), apart from a chlorine atom replacing its branched methyl group. DuPont purchased the patent rights from the University of Notre Dame, and handed the project to Wallace Carothers. He then worked with Nieuwland and took over commercial development of Nieuwland's discovery. In April 1930, the polymer was synthesised by one of Carothers' team, Arnold Collins. The polymer, named μ-polychloroprene, had the 'rubbery' properties which had been envisaged, but resembled vulcanised rubber rather than natural rubber.

POLYCHLOROPRENE

Further experiments produced a material— polychloroprene—that was closer to natural rubber. This could be milled, compounded, shaped, and turned into the μ-form by heating. The addition of metal oxides accelerated the process. This new material was far more resistant to oil and chemicals than natural rubber, although it was inferior in other ways. It went into production in 1931 as Neoprene, DuPont's trade name, and was the first commercially successful synthetic rubber polymer. Neoprene was used as latex for coatings or dipping, as well as being coagulated like natural rubber, producing a dry material. Neoprene was used widely in the automotive industry for gaskets, belting and hoses, although now it is being superseded in these applications by newer elastomers. Neoprene was used for lining tanks which would contain strong organic and inorganic acids. Wetsuits are one of the major uses for neoprene today.

Polythene (polyethylene) was the result of a serendipitous discovery at ICI, Winnington, where scientists were undertaking a series of high-pressure reaction experiments. In 1933, they were carrying out an experiment: reacting benzaldehyde with ethylene gas. A leak in the high-pressure apparatus meant that more ethylene gas, containing a small amount of oxygen, entered. This acted as a catalyst, converting some of the ethylene into polyethylene, and a white waxy substance was found. Initially they did not recognise what they had made and, because of the danger of the high-pressure experiments, they were unable to work very much with this discovery until 1935. However, in 1935, they produced the first pound of polyethylene. One of the key scientists, Eric Fawcett, presented his discovery at an international conference. This discovery mainly met with disbelief, notably from no less a person than the eminent German scientist, Herman Staudinger, who did not believe it was possible to polymerise ethylene. The first 100-tons-per-year polythylene plant went into production in 1939, just as the Second World War broke out. By this point ICI understood what they had discovered, and also the superior insulating properties of polythene. The manufacturing process of polythylene was put under a D notice—meaning top secret—and was to be produced purely for the military. Polythylene then played an important role as an insulating material for radar cables.

After the Second World War, ICI began to explore new uses for their product such as washing up bowls, buckets and babies' baths. Later polythene dolls and bottles were developed, first marketed by ICI under the name Alketh, and then Alkathene. Polythene is the name used by DuPont, who later used the trade name, Alathon.

American engineer and entrepreneur, Earl Tupper, manipulated polythene waste to produce his own 'Poly-T' polythene. He used it to manufacture Tupperware, patented in 1947, one of the most familiar types of plastic object in the world. Earl Tupper's new containers revolutionised kitchenware. The airtight seal relied on polythene's flexibility and molecular memory, producing what the Tupperware Corporation called a "vermin and insect-proof" container. Tupperware helped make plastic popular again, after the glut of shoddy and badly designed goods available in the 1940s.

PACKAGING

Polythene's biggest role, perhaps, had been in packaging—it was the material used to make the plastic bag. First developed in 1950, polythene packaging has now grown into a multi-million pound industry. Today, new types of polythene are being developed to make more sustainable and more degradable packaging. On the other side of the coin, polythene also gained a role in early implant surgery, where it was used to make the acetabular caps in an artificial hip joint. This medical procedure is still in application today.

TUPPERWARE HELPED MAKE PLASTIC POPULAR AGAIN, AFTER THE GLUT OF SHODDY AND BADLY DESIGNED GOODS AVAILABLE IN THE 1940S

New types of polythylene have been developed and, in 1953, Italian chemist, Professor Giulio Natta, and German chemist, Professor Karl Ziegler, produced high-density polythene. This polythene was created using catalysts in a method named the Ziegler-Natta process, and the new form was tougher than the earlier low density form produced by ICI during the 1930s. The difference between high and low density polyethylene depends on the molecular weight.

The more recently applied, Phillips Standard Oil (Indiana) process produces very high-density polythylenes. High-density polyethylene (HDPE) is produced using lower pressures and temperatures than those used for the ICI high pressure process, as well as by using catalysts. As well as being stiffer, high-density polyethylene is more temperature resistant than the low density form, and not flexible. The more rigid high-density form of polythylene is used for dustbins and stackable boxes, and has even been used in hip replacements. Special-grade polythene was developed to make Astroturf although now there are two more types made of nylon. New generations of polythylene are now being developed based on metallocene catalysts, and today ultra high molecular weight polythylene has been produced.

Extrusion and blow moulding were used to make polythene bottles and, in the 1950s, the company, Cascelloid, were the first to produce these. Making a polythene bottle begins with extruding a small finger-shaped piece of plastic called a parison. This piece is put into the mould and gas is injected into it, blowing the parison into the shape of the mould. Early problems were experienced with achieving a uniform thickness of the moulding, but this was resolved by varying the thickness of the parison. Today the process of making bottles involves blow moulding or injection moulding.

Although today around 60 million tons of polythene (or polyethylene) are produced every year, the earliest polyethylene fibres were made at the end of the Second World War. ICI produced a yarn called Courlene, made by Courtaulds. The immediate problem was Courlene's low melting point, which meant it could not be ironed, and was therefore difficult to use as a fabric. Polyethylene can be used for car upholstery, and has also been used for protective clothing for people who are in contact with corrosive chemicals, as it is chemically resistant as well as not water absorbent or prone to fungal attack. Polyethylene is also used as interlinings for collars and cuffs, and combined with cotton. Melted polyethylene, on the other hand, is spun through a multi-hole jet, and then solidified in cold water in a bath lying immediately below the jet. It is usual for the filaments to be drawn out to many times their original length.

THIS PAGE: Injection moulding machines. The manufacturing technique is used for making parts from both thermoplastic and thermosetting plastic materials in production. Molten plastic is injected at high pressure into a mould, which is the inverse of the product's shape. After a product is designed, moulds are made by a mouldmaker (or toolmaker) from metal, usually either steel or aluminium, and precision-machined to form the features of the desired part.

Injection moulding is widely used for manufacturing a variety of parts, from the smallest component to entire body panels of cars, and is the most common method of plastic production, with some commonly made items including bottle caps and outdoor furniture.

OPPOSITE: Plastic stackable chair, 1962–63. The injection-moulded polythene shell, designed by Robin Day, is contoured for comfort. They are also easy to store and lightweight, and thus perfect for use in schools, public places, and auditoriums.

EARLY PROBLEMS WERE
EXPERIENCED WITH
ACHIEVING A UNIFORM
THICKNESS OF THE
MOULDING, BUT THIS
WAS RESOLVED BY VARYING
THE THICKNESS OF THE
PARISON. TODAY THE
PROCESS OF MAKING
BOTTLES INVOLVES
BLOW MOULDING OR
INJECTION MOULDING

NYLON

A key plastic entering on the scene in the 1930s was nylon. Following 11 years of research and $27 million of investment, nylon was invented by Wallace Carothers, the little-known Julian Hill, and 200 other people working for DuPont in America. Patented in 1935, nylon was a replacement for expensive and fragile silk. Nylon was finally produced by combining Carothers' dedicated research, looking at the fundamental structure of polymers with Hill's pioneering method of drawing strands of nylon fibre out of a beaker. The team was led by Wallace Hume Carothers who, although a brilliant chemist, suffered from clinical depression and who was to commit suicide in 1937, before his invention, nylon, was revealed to the world. Produced in various forms, DuPont initially concentrated on Nylon 6,6—the name specifying the atomic structure of the molecule. Other types of nylon which have since proved commercially successful include Nylon 6; 6,10 and 11. The numbers refer to the number of carbon atoms in the nylon molecule.

Nylon's first public appearance was in the form of the bristles on the Miracle Tuft toothbrush in 1938. Surveys among Americans have revealed that nylon is the plastics invention they could least do without. Nylon is a tough plastic, appearing in a variety of forms, and can be made into applications as diverse as ball bearings, curtain fittings, parachutes and stockings. The first nylon stockings were made in America in February 1939, and, during the same year, DuPont licensed ICI to develop nylon in Britain and the Commonwealth. ICI and Courtaulds formed British Nylon Spinners in 1940, but for the next five years production was dedicated to wartime needs. In America, nylon was taken out of commercial production in 1942, and used by the military for parachutes and tents. Nylon stockings became an immediate hit with the

because I want my swimsuit to have (and to hold) a magnificent shape...

it's nylon

or nothing

She knows one thing. For a suit that's all shape, cling, fit...that holds attention and holds its lines...there's nothing like nylon. And she's learning something else. Today's nylon is better than ever...finer, stronger, longer-lasting. Behind this news there's an important fact: today, a good share of nylon yarn is the product of a new maker, a new standard of perfection, a new and completely integrated plant. The new brand: Chemstrand nylon.

SWIMSUIT BY CLAIRE McCARDELL
AT LORD & TAYLOR
NEW YORK
BURDINE'S, INC.
MIAMI, FLA & BRANCHES
JENNS, INC.
CINCINNATI, OHIO
JULIUS GARFINCKEL & CO.
WASHINGTON, D. C.
MONTALDO'S
ALL STORES
AND FINE STORES
EVERYWHERE

Chemstrand makes only the yarn; America's finest mills and manufacturers do the rest.
THE CHEMSTRAND CORPORATION, 350 Fifth Ave., N. Y. 1 • Plants: CHEMSTRAND® NYLON—Pensacola, Fla. • ACRILAN® ACRYLIC FIBER—Decatur, Ala.

OPPOSITE: Original Chemstrand Nylon advertising.

RIGHT: Preparing a warp from nylon yarn, British Nylon Spinners Ltd., Pontypool, 1957. Photograph by Maurice Broomfield.

SURVEYS AMONG AMERICANS HAVE REVEALED THAT NYLON IS THE PLASTICS INVENTION THEY COULD LEAST DO WITHOUT

American female consumer, so much so that there were nylon riots in 1940. Betty Grable, the Hollywood film star of the 1940s was used to model the stockings on her million dollar legs! A pair of her nylons recently sold at auction for $40,000. Glamour had come to the masses, as up to this point, women either wore silk stockings, which were very expensive, or otherwise had to make do with wool, cotton or Rayon stockings. Due to fabric shortages and rationing, British women in the war years often did not wear stockings at all, as "nylons" were very rare, instead drawing imitation nylon stocking seams on the backs of their legs.

Nylon is tough, oil and fuel resistant, with a low friction coefficient. Very strong but light, nylon is wear resistant, springs back into shape, and is not open to fungal or insect attack. Thermoplastic in nature, nylon can be injection-moulded, rotational-moulded and extruded. In industry, nylon is used in a solid form to make gears and bearings and medical sutures. The moulded variety is very tough and light so that, with its low coefficient of friction, it can be used to make zips, curtain rails and Velcro, which was invented in 1948. By the late 1940s, DuPont was producing over 1,100 different grades of nylon.

Until 1938, nylon was known by the name of Fibre 66, because each molecule had six carbon atoms attached to it. A special committee considered more than 400 names, including Carotheron and Wacara in honour of its inventor, before deciding on Nylon. This is erroneously considered to be a conjunction of New York (NY) and London (LON), but considered by Jeffrey Meikle, an authority on American plastics, to be a descendant of Nuron.

PERSPEX

A glass-like acrylic resin was first formed by Rudolph Fittig, in 1877, and developed by the German chemist, Otto Rohm. In 1928, Rohm and Haas produced acrylic commercially and at first the resin was used in coatings. Rowland Hill and John Crawford, working at ICI, produced the harder form of acrylic in 1934. ICI called the transparent form of acrylic Perspex and the trade name was registered on 16 November, 1934. The material was sold commercially by 1936. The name was derived from the Latin verb, *perspicare*, meaning "to see through". The German equivalent to Perspex was Plexiglas.

Transparent acrylic was to play an important role as a replacement for glass canopies in aircraft. The Spitfire had a characteristic vacuum-formed cockpit canopy. Surgeon, Harold Ridley, noticed that Perspex cockpit splinters, lodged in the eyes of wounded Spitfire pilots, did not trigger rejection by their bodies when these canopies shattered. Acrylic is inert, and based on carbon and hydrogen, making it highly compatible with human tissue. From this came work on developing acrylic contact lenses, to replace the existing glass versions, and also acrylic corneas. In 1949 Ridley implanted the first acrylic lens into a patient's eye, pioneering the use of plastic implants in the body.

Acrylic dentures were introduced in the 1930s. Since then acrylic has been used for medical and cosmetic purposes anywhere plastic comes into contact with the body. From the 1960s acrylic has been used in femoral implants and early micro-corneal implants, as well as for modern false nails.

After the war, uses of acrylic included the magnifying lens for the earliest (and very small) television screens. Acrylic was used to make transparent figurative sculpture, created by the late Arthur Fleischmann, and see-through architectural models. In the 1960s, acrylic was often used to make brightly coloured Pop art jewellery, an example being the Optik Art series made by jeweller Wendy Ramshaw. By the 1970s David Watkins was making

BELOW: During a hip replacement operation, the ball and socket joint are replaced with a metal prosthesis and a plastic spacer made of polythene. The plastic spacer replaces cartilage, allowing a smooth surface for movement.

OPPOSITE TOP: Traditional Perspex goggles with an air vent and elastic strap. Goggles are commonly used for snorkeling, scientific experiments, aviation and skiing.

OPPOSITE BOTTOM: Acrylic dentures, 1955–1965. The acrylic dentures were kept in an acrylic box for demonstration purposes. Image courtesy of Science and Society.

FOLLOWING PAGES: BIC's disposable razors have provided a cheap alternative to the commercial razor. Useful for travel, and emergencies, the disposable razor provides an efficient short-term shave.

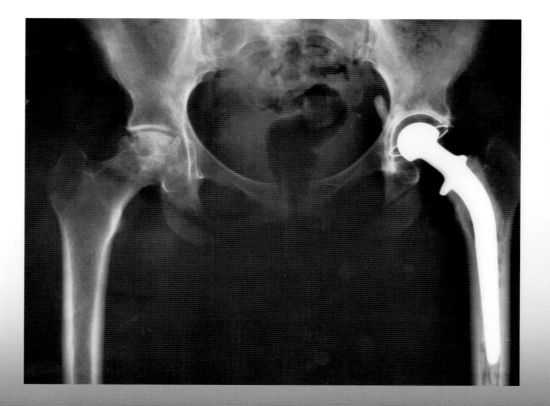

designer acrylic necklaces that were modern and simple in design yet high value pieces.

A common use for acrylic today is in moulded bathroom and light fittings, car taillights, and some of the world's largest windows. It is also found in artist and house paints, outdoor signs, baths, as a fibre in fake fur coats and in 1960s table tops.

Acrylic sheet (polymethyl methacrylate or PMMA) was made by heating the monomer, methyl methacrylate, into heavy syrup which was poured in between flat glass sheets (giving acrylic its highly polished surface). The glass "cell" was placed in an oven, to complete the polymerisation process, removed, cooled, and had the glass plates removed. The manufacturing process of Perspex was difficult, as the syrup could react violently, bubbles could appear in the cast sheets, and any dust or worker's sweat had to be removed using spatulas. According to industry insider Bob Whitesell, most of the acrylic sold by German manufacturer Rohm and Hass after the Second World War, went to make, "poorly fabricated... geegaws and gimcracks".

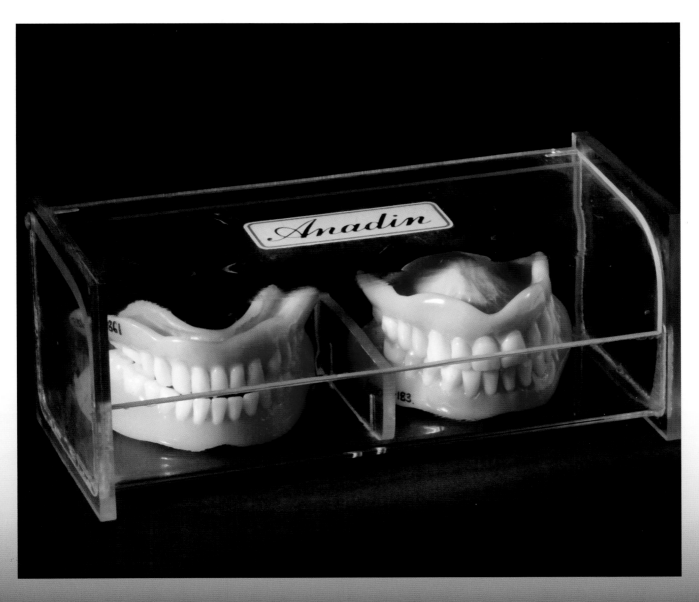

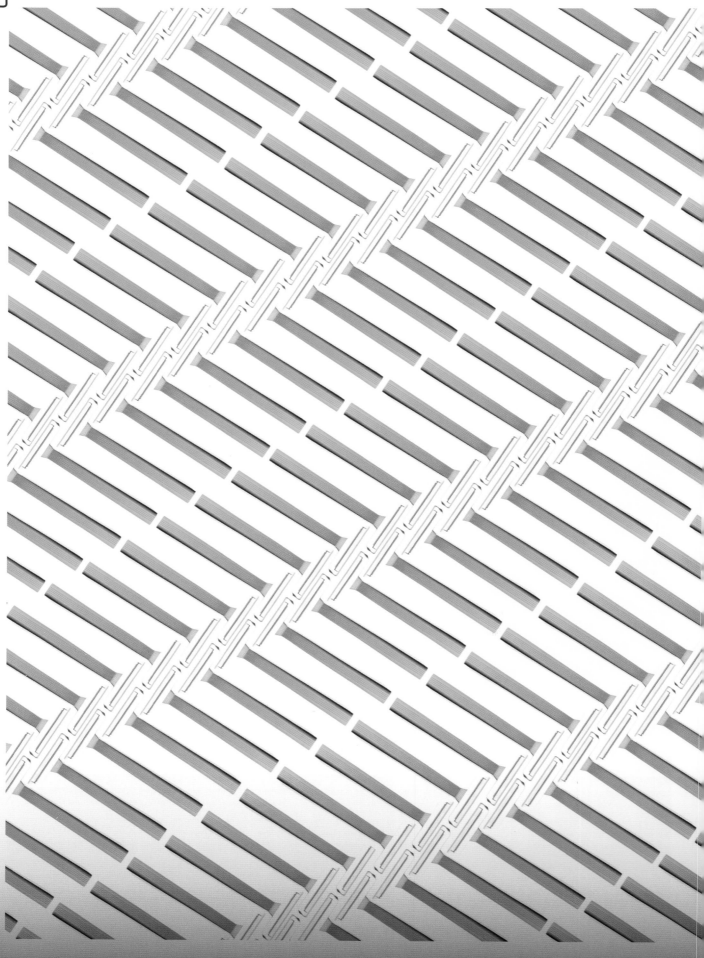

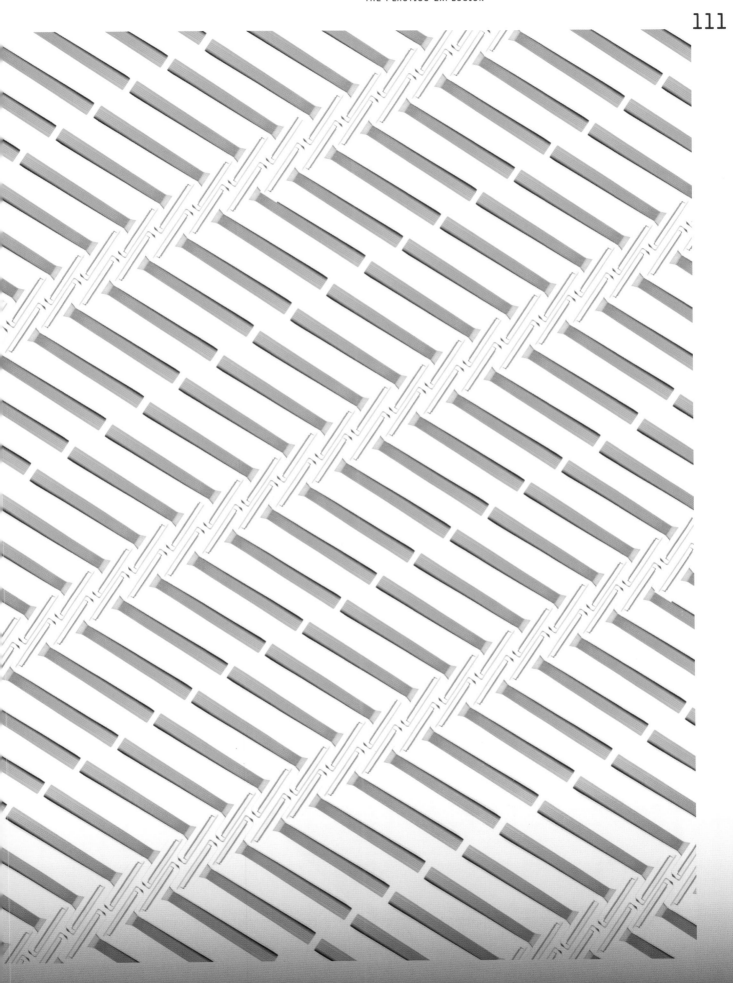

BELOW: Brooch mimicking the paint palette of an artist.

OPPOSITE: Tatty Devine's laser-cut pink sunglasses badge.

Tatty Devine is famous for unique and quirky accessories, which elevate jewellery to art status.

TATTY DEVINE

Reviving jewellery in the twenty-first century Harriet Vine and Rosie Wolfenden, the two designers behind Tatty Devine, use plastic as a trademark material to create accessories with unique and memorable designs.

Tatty Devine designs are quirky, tongue-in-cheek and kitsch. Among their themes, they combine English eccentricity, fairy tales, 1950s Americana and pop music. Re-appropriating designs of iconic objects and images, Tatty Devine creates pieces which are appealing and classic. They use a laser cutting process to cut acrylic, a method which is convenient, efficient and quick, and allows for intricate designs to be realised. Clean lines, and two-dimensional cutting creates the trademark 'flat look' of their pieces. In the same way the clean bright and chunky acrylic material holds the bold message that their designs require.

Tatty Devine have recently collaborated with big names, such as Gilbert and George, Rob Ryan and Tate Gallery, London, thus combining design, craft, culture, fine art and a glimmer of comedy into their pieces. Tatty Devine's classic pieces include the Piano Keys necklace and the Heart Glasses necklace. Innovative collaboration with the Tate resulted in the Swatch necklace, which references industrial colour swatches from acrylic pantone reference books. The colours symbolise different art movements for example 'Pop art' red, 'Minimalism' white and 'Bauhaus' blue. Large chunks of laser cut acrylic in their respective colours become a page in a mini art historical reference book. Each piece is made in the Tatty Devine studio, London.

Aware of the consequences of using plastics in the now environmentally aware climate, the majority of Tatty Devine's materials are recycled. Bringing kitsch back into fashion, each piece has a timeless quality. Like the Celluloid accessories of the early twentieth century, plastics replace the more expensive gold and silver, allowing for the growth of a more disposable fashion industry. The lightweight characteristic of plastic, and the vast availability of colours permit designs to be more courageous. Tatty Devine jewellery utilises these characteristics of plastic to its advantage, creating a modern, clean and unique product.

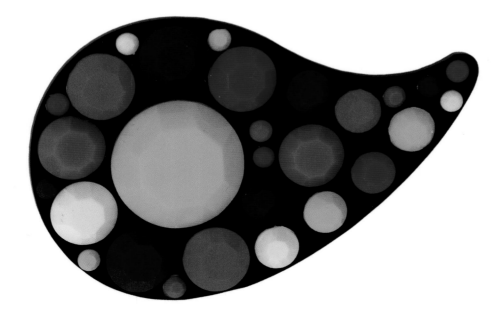

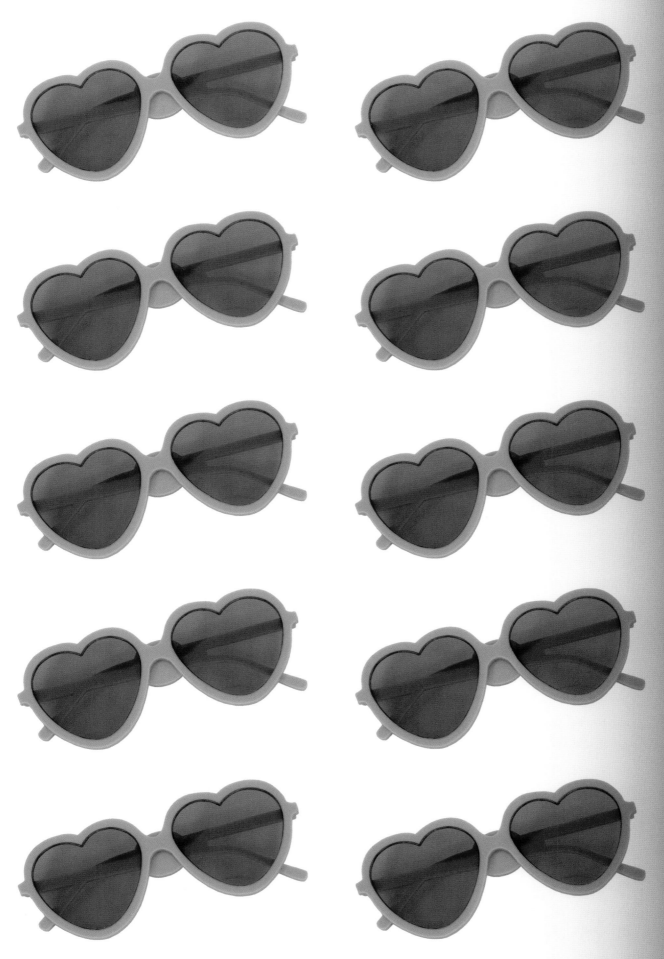

PVC

Polyvinyl chloride (PVC) is polymerised from the monomer, vinyl chloride, and can be produced in a range of hardnesses: from very soft to very hard. In its original state, polyvinyl chloride was first recorded in 1835 by the French chemist, Henri Regnault. The plastic was polymerised in 1872, and in 1912, created in a soft plasticised form in Moscow by I Ostromislensky. America's first PVC had been manufactured by 1928 and it was not until 1939 that Britain followed suit. The Second World War forced developments and a PVC factory was built at Hillhouse by 1940. During the war, PVC was a significant material, used for electrical insulation, and replacing rubber fixtures in aircraft, radio and electrical goods. Under the name Vinylite (a copolymer of vinyl chloride and vinyl acetate), developed by Union Carbide, PVC was later adopted in 1948 as the material for gramophone records and, due to its superior qualities, had largely replaced shellac within five years.

PVC has been utilised in a variety of ways, ranging from inflatable chairs and designer wear in the 1960s, to waterproof macs and fruit bowls. In the 1960s PVC became synonymous with the space age, and was also used for structural applications such as pipes, guttering and windows and for wipeable wallpaper and packaging. PVC is employed as a copolymer with acetate to make records, although this may become a defunct process. It is also used in packaging, for example in bottle tops or closures.

Easy to modify, PVC is one of the most versatile plastics, but the additives and plasticisers that make PVC flexible have caused problems, giving off toxic fumes when incinerated. Today, unlike the 1960s, the additives in consumer plastics are carefully regulated. In contrast to the toxic fumes, PVC has many life-saving medical uses, such as blood bags. During the Second

EASY TO MODIFY, PVC IS ONE OF THE MOST VERSATILE PLASTICS

TOP: PVC is the most widely used thermoplastic material in medical devices because it is deemed safe, chemically stable and inert. It is also extremely versatile and easily fabricated. Medical products made from PVC are usable inside the body, easy to sterilise and simple to assemble into products. PVC is also used in clothing for those in medical professions.

BOTTOM: PVC Gardener, 1970. Sophia Pienkos, a gardener at London's Royal Botanical Gardens, Kew, wears a new space-age, transparent PVC suit for protection when using toxic sprays in the tropical house. Photograph by Keystone. Courtesy of Getty Images.

World War, Dr Carl Walter was frustrated by the glass bottles used to store and transport blood supplies to the front. These often broke in transit and were difficult to carry and, as a result, many lives were lost. Walter's new lightweight and durable PVC blood bag was tested during the 1950s Korean War. The successful design is still in use today.

PVC is the most common plastic used for making toys today, including Barbie dolls. 'Born' in 1959, Barbie was one of the first dolls to have an adult body, delighting 1950s girls and horrifying many parents. Now, with three Barbies sold every second, has the doll become a victim of her own success? Dr Agnes Nairn of Bath University asked 100 children what they thought. Most had "a box full of Barbies... to them, Barbie has come to symbolise excess. Barbies are not special, they are disposable".

Mary Quant was among the first fashion designers to work with plastic. Her Wet Collection, made from PVC, caused a sensation in 1963. Quant recalls the problems she faced trying to weld and sew this "revolutionary new material" together. "We fell down all along the line on production. It was disastrous. Everyone wanted our things and we did not know how to make them." Vinyl records and fetish clothing may have given PVC cult status, but around half of all global production is for construction, especially uPVC window frames and pipes.

BARBIE WAS ONE OF THE FIRST DOLLS TO HAVE AN ADULT BODY

118

POLYURETHANE

Polyurethane was discovered, in Germany, 1937, by Dr Otto Bayer and his team. Bayer continued to work with polyurethane, developing a variety of foams as well as coatings, glues and fibres. By the 1960s, Polyurethane was being used by state of the art furniture designers, such as Roger Tallon who, in 1969, made his spectacular Super Chair with an egg box, profile-cut surface, manufactured by Jacques Lacloche, Paris. A flexible and versatile plastic, polyurethane is also strong and resilient. It can be elastic, rigid or foamed and has good impact resistance.

As foam, polyurethane is used to pad out mattresses and sofas and to make carpet underlay. Polyurethane's protective properties make it useful for coatings, packaging, padding and car bumpers, as well as earplugs and refrigerator insulation, and clothing. It can be melted (thermoplastic) or can be a thermoset.

Polyurethane foam was used to make television puppets of the 1970s, such as Larry the Lamb. The foam was important in the development of 'low-level living' G-Plan furniture, launched in 1953, as well as being adopted by a range of other furniture designers. Unfortunately polyurethane foam degrades over time and crumbles, so preserving these early icons of design and television history is proving very challenging.

SPANDEX

Polyurethane is used as an ingredient in spandex. Spandex can stretch up to 600 per cent and still recover its original shape. It is the material of choice for superheroes and athletes, as well as technical corsets and underwear. Invented in the 1950s, spandex is a copolymer—a plastic made from two different monomer building blocks. Spandex is also known as elastane and Lycra. As one ingredient in Lycra, polyurethane brought us this new stretch fabric in 1959. Lycra has revolutionised leisure and sportswear and a variety of clothing to ensure comfortable fitting. Playtex produced its extra comfortable Lycra bra in 1959. Although many superheroes pre-date the invention of spandex, the uncommonly tight clothing most superheroes wear has indelibly linked them to the material. Plastic Man, portrayed in the eponymous comic dated to 1966, is perhaps the ultimate of all superheroes—as flexible and elastic as the spandex costumes he wears.

Polyurethane is also used in an alternative type of female condom for those who have an allergy to latex. They are increasingly popular worldwide: the number of female condoms distributed annually in South Africa alone rose from 1.2 to 3 million between 2003 and 2006.

Polyurethane was used for the first fully synthetic World Cup football in 1986. The highly technical, 2006 ball had a polyurethane skin, making it far more abrasion, weather and water resistant, and an elastic, rather than leather ball. The ball also broke with tradition, by having 14 polyurethane surface panels instead of 32, to make it, according to the manufacturer Adidas, the roundest football ever developed. Modern World Cup Match footballs have a polyurethane skin and almost perfectly spherical shape, to give strikers more control. The centre is latex with a glass fibre hard shell.

Test spraying foam insulation, Shell International, 1963. Here a worker in protective clothing sprays polyurethane insulation material in a leaky cow barn at Woodstock Farm. The photograph was taken by Maurice Broomfield, who recorded British industry's recovery after the Second World War. Broomfield's images reflect the idea of a utopian relationship between humans and machines. Image courtesy of Science and Society.

FOLLOWING PAGES: Latex condoms are stronger, thinner and last longer than their rubber predecessors. Today, both male and female condoms are available. Although most condoms are made from latex, polyurethane and lambskin condoms are also widely available. As a method of contraception, condoms are inexpensive, easy to use, have few side effects, and have the advantage of offering protection against sexually transmitted diseases.

SPANDEX CAN STRETCH UP TO 600 PER CENT AND STILL RECOVER ITS ORIGINAL SHAPE

NEIL ZAKIEWICZ

Sculpture, of all the arts, derives value from its sense of permanence, so when London artist, Neil Zakiewicz, re-interpreted classical sculptures using foam rather than stone, both their physical and metaphysical gravitas were unburdened. Replacing sculpture's heavy and hard marble and metal with upholstery foam—a material better suited to home than gallery—is not just a superficial adjustment but one which challenges the traditions and pomp of high art.

Zakiewicz's art is surprising and pleasurable for just this reason. Each piece is a mockery of classical sculptural forms—like the oversized, raised fist of the Socialist Realist movement, or wall-mounted animal heads to commemorate a hunt—but instead of shaping marble or performing taxidermy, Zakiewicz carves his forms from soft polyurethane foam—the type you would find stuffed into the pillows of a sofa.

One of Zakiewicz's earlier shows, *Monumental*, was a tongue in cheek reference to classical stone sculpture. The work debunked artistic authority by re-interpreting its traditional materials and subjects. Here, the giant carved fists, which Social Realists used to represent gestures of power, become instead the artist's hands. *Pencil Holder*, imagines the iconic raised fist of power awkwardly brandishing a bunch of pencils. It looks similar to classical white stone or marble, but the white foam is podgy and soft and shifts when you touch it. The inappropriate material and altered narrative subvert the iconic raised fist. It sags beneath the weight of its massive wooden pencils. Instead of being forbidding and austere, the piece is ridiculous.

Upholstery foam is the nemesis of stone: where stone is hard and heavy and permanent, upholstery foam is a generous and giving material, designed to adapt and reshape every time you lean on it. The uncanny visual similarity between foam and marble belies their many tactile differences and sets the scene for the broken expectations which are fundamental to Zakiewicz's work.

Zakiewicz treats foam sculpturally, using techniques like carving and chiselling to shape it and supporting the shapes with built-in wooden struts. Like the other plastics, foam is characterised by a willingness to be manipulated, a plasticity which responds well to shaping, but the rough hewn edges of Zakiewicz's sculptures (which he has cut into with a bread knife) lack the perfection of moulded plastic forms or the smoothness of classical sculpture.

Where a stone sculpture commemorates, a sponge sculpture softens. The more serious the iconography, the sillier it seems in sponge. Unlike stone, foam is porous and seems almost to breathe. Its unique ability to hold and shift its shape was designed for comfort rather than permanence. There is an irony in these spongy sculptures, which offer only slight resistance to touch. Using the internal material of a couch rebels against high art and its associated authority which, in Zakiewicz's work (like the sculptures themselves) seems to buckle under its own weight.

TOP: *Pencil Holder*, 2005. Image
courtesy Neil Zakiewicz.

BOTTOM: *Wolf*, 2003. Image
courtesy of Neil Zakiewicz.

POLYSTYRENE

Introduced in the 1930s, polystyrene is a synthetic plastic that has often had a bad press. It is lightweight, easy to shape, good for insulating, and is popular for throwaway products, from the infamous expanded-polystyrene cup and fast food containers, to toothbrushes, biros and disposable razors. In 1866 PE Marcelin Bertholet showed that polystyrene could be made from styrene (a derivative of benzene and ethylene). In 1930, IG Farben produced polystyrene on a commercial scale, known by 1935, as Trolitul. In 1937 polystyrene was being made in America under the names Styron (from the Dow Chemical company) and Bakelite polystyrene (from the Bakelite Corporation).

Although polystyrene was fashionable for tableware in the late 1940s, many early products were brittle and tended to crack. Polystyrene can be brightly coloured, initially making it suitable for decorative boxes, jewellery, food containers, picnic utensils and electrical insulators. Later modifications of polystyrene brought improved properties, and polystyrene has found uses in a huge range of products, including Airfix models and toys, furniture, packaging and radio cabinets. Due to its optical clarity, polystyrene is also used today in medical and industrial probes. Expanded polystyrene is an excellent packaging material and insulant.

Fast food chain, McDonald's, originally adopted expanded polystyrene packaging to reduce the time taken to get burgers to customers, and to keep them hot. Growing public anxiety in the 1980s about increasing litter, the slow degradability of many plastics, and concern about the ozone-depleting chlorofluorocarbons (CFCs) used for expanded polystyrene at the time, forced McDonald's to rethink and move back to bulky paperboard packaging.

OPPOSITE: Mountains of polystyrene, a polymer made from the monomer styrene, a liquid hydrocarbon that is commercially manufactured from petroleum by the chemical industry. Polystyrene is a thermoplastic substance, normally existing in solid state at room temperature, but melting if heated (for moulding or extrusion), and becoming solid again on cooling.

Pure solid polystyrene is a colourless, hard plastic with limited flexibility. It can be cast into moulds with fine detail. Polystyrene can be transparent or can be made to take on various colours. It is economical and is used for producing plastic model assembly kits, license plate frames, plastic cutlery, and many other objects where a fairly rigid, economical plastic is desired.

TOP AND BOTTOM: Warhammer Giant, by Citadel, 2008. The model kit shown before assembly and completed prior to painting. Model assembled Tobias Redding.

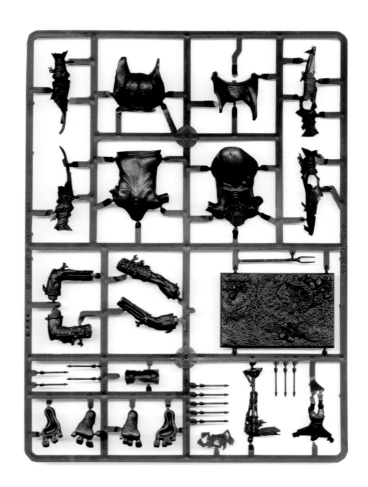

POLYSTYRENE IS EASY TO SHAPE, GOOD FOR INSULATING, AND IS POPULAR FOR THROWAWAY PRODUCTS

A chewed polystyrene cup on a cafe table surrounded by plastic bottled condiments and a plastic lid and spoon. Polystyrene is a good insulator, and is therefore suitable for retaining the heat in hot beverages. Courtesy of Getty Images.

OPPOSITE: A man on ice skates demonstrating a movement on artificial ice made of Teflon. Photograph by Ted Russell for Time Life Pictures. Courtesy of Getty Images.

Industrial products made with Teflon fluoropolymer resins have excellent resistance to high temperatures, chemical reaction, corrosion, and stress-cracking.

BELOW: Tom Dixon giving away hundreds of chairs to the British public from Trafalgar Square, 2005.

Dixon is a English industrial designer—one of the few designers without formal training. Dixon began designing furniture in his early 20s, creating a variety of objects including the S-bend Chair. The Chair was discovered later by Italian furniture maker Cappellini. Since then, Dixon has produced many products, the most notable of which are the Mirrorball light and Soft System couch. He currently is the head of design at Finnish company Artek and also engages in many design-focused speaking events around the globe. Dixon is a champion of sustainable design, and does not believe students need degrees to succeed as designers, suggesting that the key to success is to simply make something unique and desirable.

TOM DIXON

Tom Dixon is a modern designer who finds innovative uses for plastics. In 2006 he designed and displayed 500 polystyrene chairs in Trafalgar Square, turning it into the biggest living room in Britain. In what has become known as "The Great Chair Grab", the chairs were given away at the end of the day. The chairs were made from expanded polystyrene (EPS), best known for packaging. This innovative giveaway was made in the hope that others might be inspired to design with polystyrene. Dixon said: "EPS is incredibly lightweight and totally versatile—unique amongst plastics; a designer gets the unusual opportunity of working in large solid volumes" and "Making a polystyrene chair has given me the opportunity to fulfil an ambition to make design available to all; this time literally, by giving away hundreds of these chairs to Londoners—absolutely, no chains attached, 100 per cent FREE!"

TEFLON

Polyethyltetrafluorethene (PTFE), otherwise known as Teflon, was discovered by accident by Dr Roy Plunkett at DuPont, in 1938. The first pilot plant for Teflon opened in 1943. Teflon has become synonymous with non-stick saucepans, and was first developed for military and industrial applications. It has been used in space suits and satellite arrays, due to its toughness, combined with its heat-resistant properties. In 1969, the first man on the moon, Neil Armstrong, wore a spacesuit with Teflon seals.

GORE-TEX is an early example of an engineered fibre. A waterproof and breathable fabric, it is used to make outdoor clothing. Made up of a layer of porous PTFE sandwiched in between two layers of nylon, GORE-TEX was invented by Americans Wilbert L Gore, Rowena Taylor, and Robert W Gore and patented in 1976. The microstructure of the porous PTFE is made of nodes interconnected by fibrils. In Britain PTFE was developed under the trade name Fluon by ICI, and as Hostaflon by Hoechst in Germany.

BELOW: Volivik Bic biro
chandelier by enPieza.

OPPOSITE: The ubiquitous biro.

BIRO

As polystyrene is light, relatively cheap and can be transparent, it was a good choice as a material to use to make a disposable consumer item, the Bic biro. Launched in 1950, the Bic Cristal ballpoint pen revolutionised writing. Introduced by the Société Bic company, based in France, the famous Bic slogan: "writes first time, every time" helped sales in a market flooded with cheap, unreliable ballpoint pens. The pen's plastic construction makes it easier to produce and cheaper to buy. The Bic biro's success lies in a combination of good design and disposability. Société Bic sold its 100 billionth disposable ballpoint pen in 2005.

Spanish design company enPieza has taken the reuse of plastics products to another level, with their Volivik Bic biro chandelier, produced in 2007. This is made from 347 recycled Bic Cristal pens and 347 paper clips; this chandelier is one of only 30 made as homage to a classic plastic design. The barrels of clear Bic pens are made from polystyrene.

WRITES FIRST TIME, EVERY TIME

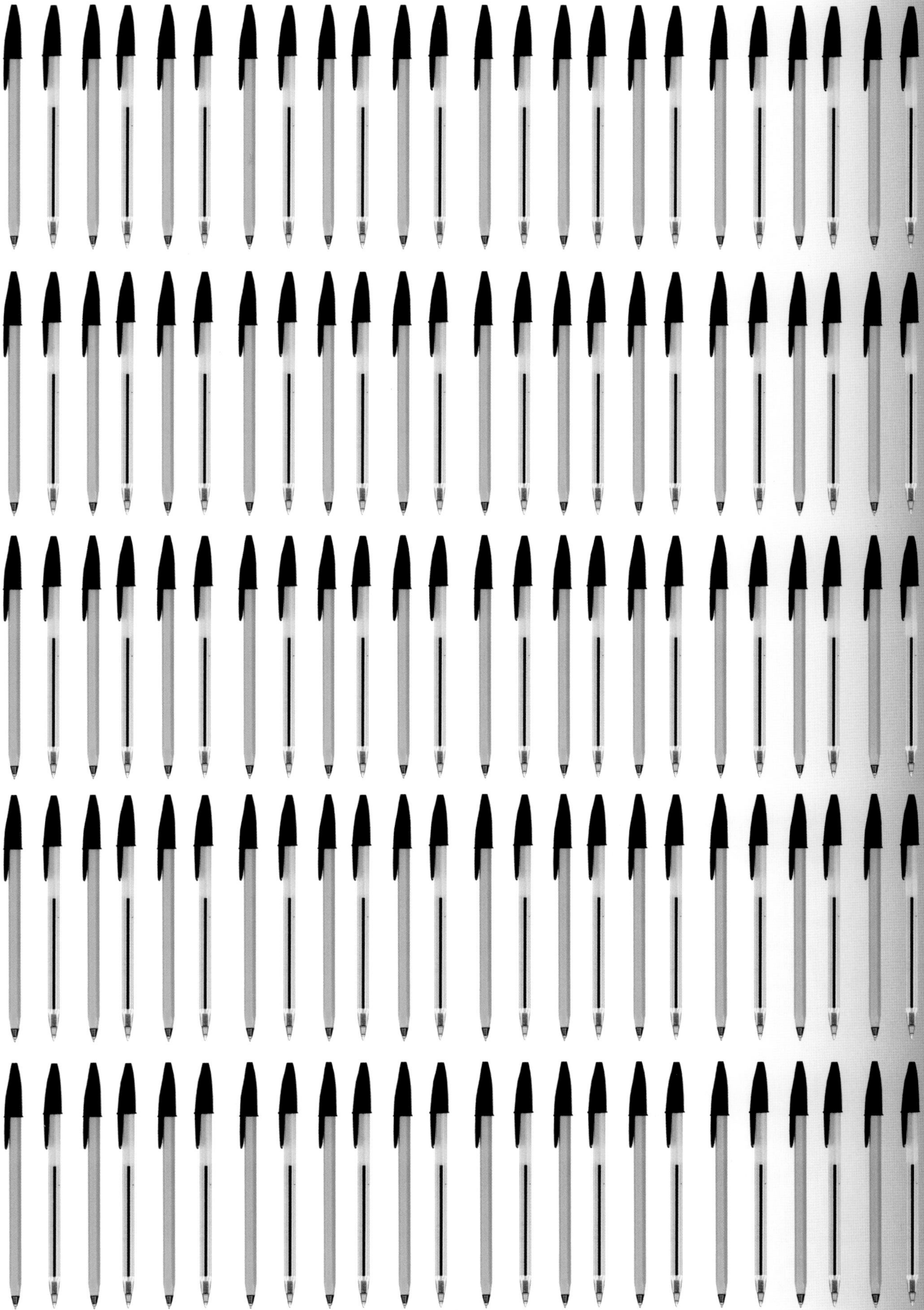

OPPOSITE: A surgeon inserting a silicone breast implant during post-cancer reconstructive breast surgery. The patient, having undergone a complete mastectomy, now has silicone to replace the removed lost body tissue. Courtesy of Getty Images.

SILICONE

Silicone is made of silicon combined with carbon, and can be produced in liquid form—for furniture polishes, paints, resins, sealants and glues—as well as in solid, rigid substances and soft gels. Initially worked on by Professor Frederick Kipping of Nottingham University in the early twentieth century, silicone's applications were explored and developed by the Corning Glass Company and the Dow Chemical Company in 1931, resulting in the formation, in 1943, of the Dow Corning Corporation for the commercial production of silicones. A silicone molecule contains a repeating silicon-oxygen backbone with organic groups attached by silicon-carbon bonds to a significant proportion of the silicon atoms.

The first silicone breast implant was pioneered in 1962. A boon to women who have suffered a mastectomy, silicone implants are now synonymous with an idea of a 'plastic', rather false, culture due to the growth in the popularity of silicone implants for cosmetic, rather than medical, reasons.

Silicone rubber (elastomer) is used for various implants such as heart valves, ears, and noses, as well as for gaskets, sealing rings and grouting. Liquid silicone rubber is used for coating wire and cable in the electrical industry. Silicone rubber has effective applications when properties, such as heat resistance and ability to function over a wide range of temperatures, are needed. Silicone polymers of appropriate weight must be cross-linked to produce elastomeric properties.

DESPITE BEING A BOON TO WOMEN WHO HAVE SUFFERED A MASTECTOMY, SILICONE IMPLANTS ARE NOW SYNONYMOUS WITH THE IDEA OF A 'PLASTIC' AND FALSE CULTURE...

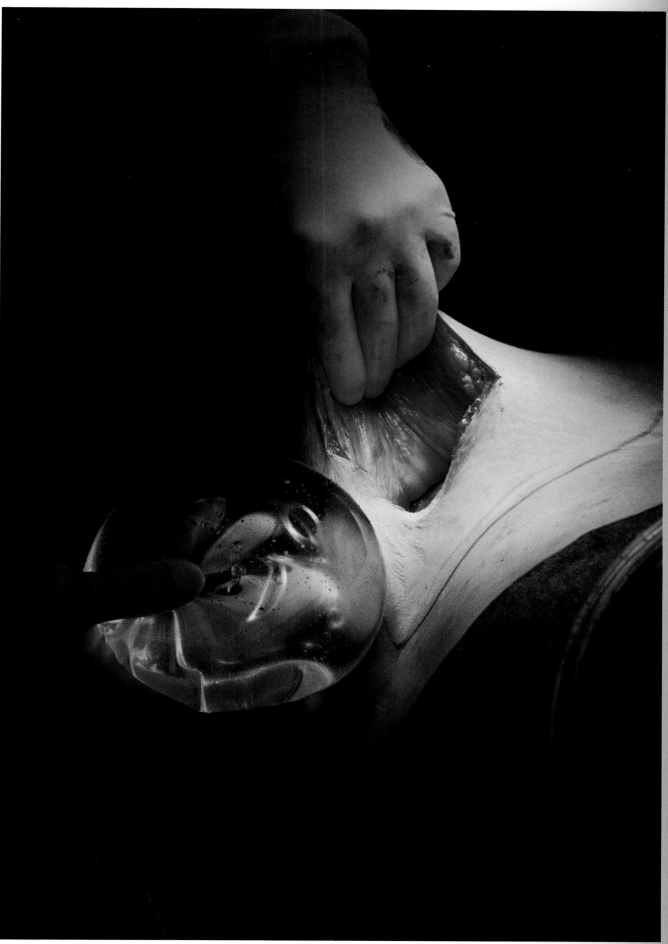

BEYOND THE 1930S

BELOW: One of NASA's Mars Exploration Rovers (MER). Glenn Research Center's Plum Brook Station in Sandusky, Ohio, played a critical role in testing the landing airbags for the MERs. The MER airbags had to be strong enough to cushion the spacecraft landing on rough terrain and to allow it to bounce across Mars' surface at freeway speeds. A test spacecraft and airbag system of about 1,180 pounds was accelerated with a bungee cord system onto a platform of rocks. The drop speed on landing was 20–24 yards per second.

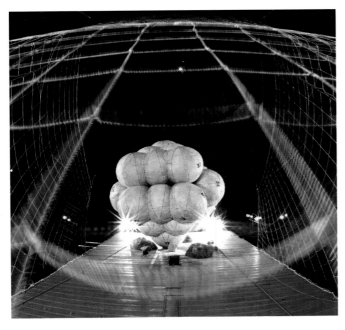

Acrylonitrile (PAN) and acrylic fibres were developed during and after the Second World War. Examples include Orlon, an acrylonitrile which was developed by DuPont, who started research in early 1940, and had progressed to the pilot plant stage by 1945. In 1948, the resultant fibre was given the trade mark Orlon, and commercial production began in 1950. The acrylic fibre, Acrilan, made by the Chemstrand Corporation, was piloted in 1950, and sold to the public in 1952. Acrylic fibres form a significant part of the synthetic fibre industry today.

POLYESTER

During his research, Wallace Carothers also worked with polyesters (polyethylene terephthalate), but discarded them in favour of polyamides (nylons), which he considered made better fibres. JR Whinfield and JT Dickson, of the Calico Printers Association in Britain, took Carothers' research further. In 1941 the pair discovered the polyester fibre, which later became known as Terylene (polyethylene terephthalate fibre). This discovery was then exploited by ICI, and polyester became the first popular hardy fabric in times of post-war austerity.

In fibre form, polyester makes quick-drying, durable, wrinkle resistant fabrics. As chemically resistant PET bottles, polyester holds sparkling drinks and water, and is seen almost everywhere today.

Cheap and easy to care for, polyester was the material of 1970s 'modern' man—ranging in products from the disco suit, to everyday leisurewear. However, polyester's poor breathability made the use of good deodorant essential. This problem was tackled with the development of high-tech engineered polyester fibres in the 1980s. In the 1970s, easy-wearing polyester two-piece leisure suits were the epitome of cool machismo, style and assurance. Polyester clothing's crease-free and shape-retaining properties were a great selling point. Brands such as denim company, Levi's 'Sta Prest'—a favourite of British mods and skinheads in the 1960s—and 'Perma Prest' are some of the best known. Perhaps John Travolta's white, three-piece polyester suit from the film, *Saturday Night Fever*, 1977, encapsulated the excesses of the 1970s disco scene.

Polyester is also used for high-tech applications in outer Space. Pathfinder's 1997 Mars landing relied on airbags made from a manipulated polyester fabric called Vectran. This was the first time airbags had helped spacecraft to land on another planet. Since the success of Pathfinder, airbags have been used for other NASA missions, including Mars Exploration, which landed two rovers on the Martian surface in 2004. Unlike conventional polyesters, the molecular chains of Vectran fibres all orientate in the same direction, making it five times stronger than steel, weight for weight—perfect properties for soaring 100–200 metres between bounces.

CHEAP POLYESTER WAS THE MATERIAL OF 1970S 'MODERN' MAN

BELOW: Fibreglass shark's head, 2008, which was designed as a wall hanging. Fibreglass is constructed from extremely fine fibres of glass. It is used as a reinforcing agent for many polymer products. The resulting composite material, properly known as fibre-reinforced polymer (FRP) or glass-reinforced plastic (GRP), is more commonly referred to as fibreglass.

OPPOSITE: Reinforced fibreglass step ladder with aluminium steps, 2008.

The polyester used in fibreglass is unsaturated and thermosetting it can have a wide range of properties, with respect to toughness and resilience. Glass has high tensile and poor compression strength, while unsaturated polyesters have the reverse. Bonding is crucial to get good interlaniar shear strength.

FIBREGLASS

A composite synthetic plastic, glass-reinforced polyester (GRP), combined polyester resin with glass fibres, making a strong, lightweight material. GRP has revolutionised the design of planes, trains and automobiles, and enabled the construction of plastic buildings and enormous wind turbine blades, as well as the one-piece chair.

As early as the second millennium BC, glass fibres were known to the ancient Egyptians, and by 1713 AD they had been woven. Glass fibres were not successfully used with resins as a composite material until the 1940s. Glass fibre reinforced plastics are used for furniture, baths, in buildings, roofing, car bodies and boat hulls. "Low pressure resins" for reinforced plastics were first used commercially in 1942, in the form of glass cloth reinforced resin radomes for aircraft in America. There were early problems with getting the polyester resin to set, but the problems associated with air inhibition and cold curing were solved by 1951.

GRP was also used for corrugated roofing, decorative mouldings and (unsuccessfully) for window frames and baths. By the late 1940s, GRP, commonly known as "fibreglass" was in use commercially, and many of the earliest developments came in the manufacture of boat bodies. By 1947, 16 foot seaplane floats had been produced in Britain. The first car with a fibreglass body, the Corvette, was made in 1953. In 1954, Singer Motors Limited produced a fibreglass-bodied roadster: the Singer SMX. This was one of the first plastic-bodied cars to be produced by a British car manufacturer.

Furniture designers began to use GRP in the late 1940s and 1950s, as the material allowed them free rein in form. Furniture styles became more flowing and organic. The classic, glass fibre, stackable chair is tough and fairly inflexible, as well as light and convenient to move around. Cars and boats also became lighter as a result, and American and European designers produced innovative GRP chairs at this time. In England, the GRP boat, Wildfire, caused a sensation by winning all the races it entered.

Glass fibre reinforced plastics are made of glass fibres bound together with polyester resin. The first polyester resin (polyglycerol tartrate) was produced in 1847 by Jön Jakob Berzelius. A variety of polyester resins now exist, but, in essence, they are all condensation polymers, produced by a variety of processes, including reacting a glycol with a dicarboxylic acid.

Two brittle materials (glass and polyester resin) make a very tough material when combined together. This is because the fibres in the resin act as crack stoppers. Certain low pressure composites such as fibre glass are made using hand lay up with chopped fibre mats and used for low value end use such as buckets and brushes. The advanced composites such as carbon fibre reinforced composites that are used in aerospace components are made with continuous fibres and cured in autoclaves.

Epoxy resins are used with glass fibre to make composite, low pressure, reinforced moulding materials. Epoxy resins were first developed in the 1930s by Pierre Castan, becoming commercially viable in 1939 with IG Farben's patent concerning liquid polyepoxides. Initially, their high production costs, compared with polyesters, limited their use until later improvements in production methods. They are particularly suitable for use in space craft, due to their light weight, combined with excellent electrical properties.

Styrene acrylonitrile copolymers have been produced since the 1940s. Tougher than styrene, they were used for various applications. However, a further modification of the material was the 1948 addition of another polymer—the synthetic rubber, butadiene—making acrylonitrile butadiene styrene (ABS). Commercially produced in the 1950s, these ABS copolymers could be made with variable properties and were also easy to process, so that ABS became the most popular engineering polymer. Tough and impact resistant ABS is used in areas where high-impact protective buffering is needed, such as school playgrounds and car bumpers.

ABS was selected by key designers Marco Zanuso and Richard Sapper to make the housing of the small but stylish Doney television set made in 1962 by Brionvega, Milan. This design won the prestigious Italian Compasso d'Oro design award.

ABS was used to make LEGO, perhaps the best known plastic toy. Developed in 1949, LEGO was first made of cellulose acetate. The ultimate first plastic Swatch watch was made in 1983, with an ABS case and a PVC strap. This was not the first plastic watch as it was preceded in 1971 by the TISSOT synthetic "Idea" watch.

Other copolymers such as high-impact polystyrene (HIPS) have been developed. To create HIPS, polybutadiene rubber is added to the polystyrene. The result is a tough, impact resistant material, a great improvement on the impact resistance properties of early polystyrene which was brittle. Now super high impact polystyrenes (SHIPS) have also been developed.

1950s

Polypropylene was first polymerised in 1954, by Giulio Natta, of high-density polythene fame. Polypropylene is used for packaging, one-piece moulded hinges, and ropes, and is now is the world's largest consumer plastic, overtaking polythene. It is tough and chemical resistant and can be produced in a variety of grades. Natta and Ziegler were awarded the Nobel prize in chemistry, 1963, for their work on producing stereo-regular polymers using organo-metallic catalysts, mainly using isotactic polypropylene.

Following the Second World War plastics manufacturers began to invest in new engineering materials. 1950s DuPont trade

literature referred to engineering materials, and the American
Celanese Corporation specifically alluded to engineering plastics
in the launch of their new acetal copolymer in 1962. The 1950s
was a period when there was the first recognition of a new class
of plastics—engineering plastics. This followed the sustained work
at DuPont in developing polymers for specific purposes and with
particular properties, beginning with the various grades of nylon
first developed in the 1930s.

The 1950s brought a new understanding of the need for light
but durable materials. Mass-production and mass-consumption of
a range of new plastics products and materials had left the market
saturated according to those who sold and promoted plastics.
The market was also recognised as conservative with a plethora
of plastics in existence. The vision emerged among American
chemical manufacturers, such as DuPont and General Electric
(GE), that future success would entail modifying existing plastics
as well as mechanically blending different polymers to give
particular properties. This new perception produced a superior
class of plastics for use in demanding applications, which had
properties tailored to their relevant engineering requirements over
a range of temperatures—whether it be strength and stiffness,
fatigue and toughness, creep, chemical resistance, or flammability
and electrical properties.

These materials could be mass-produced by injection
moulding to high tolerances, and these qualities made them
attractive with regard to both performance and cost.

Yellow, by Nathan Sawaya, circa 2007. Nathan Sawaya is a LEGO brick artist who constructs sculptures from the iconic children's toy. With more than 1.5 million coloured LEGO components in his New York studio, Sawaya's range of LEGO sculptures elevate the perception of plastic as an art material.

Just as the miniature, caricatured characters of Cake and Neave, are a humorous reference to the artists themselves, so the works they produce are scaled-down versions of iconic modern artworks and artists.

Cake and Neave's oeuvre is characterised by its odd proportions, the eclectic mix of artistic materials employed—including LEGO, Scalextric tracks, Smurfs and Pictionary—and a fascination with modern art.

In Art Craziest Nation, a miniature gallery, masterpieces of modern art are represented by three-dimensional replicas constructed from LEGO bricks.

Included in the exhibition are scaled-down, LEGO versions of pieces by Tracey Emin (pictured) and Gilbert and George, as well as Damien Hirst's formaldehyde shark tank and the Chapmans' Goya homage. Although the focus of the piece was the Young British Artist phenomenon, it also explored figureheads of the European avant-garde like Joseph Beuys and Yves Klein.

Traditional art materials give way to LEGO kits—the colourful bricks assembled into shapes which, in turn, are peopled with little LEGO figurines. Although the 'LEGOy' language and its shapes are often at odds with the original artworks, the artists make no change to the materials' natural properties, using its interlocking mechanisms and angular buildings blocks as a child would, rather than painting or remoulding them to conform more easily to the original piece.

The comment is embedded less in the minds of the artists than the material—the tension between the adult concerns of Tracey Emin's bed and the child-like LEGO aesthetic it takes on in Art Craziest Nation, reflects the serious intent of this artistic endeavour.

Cross-fertilising the simple geometry of a kid's game with the complex shapes and forms of high art captures the Little Artists' ongoing interrogation of the relationship between art and branding. Like a gallery's gift shop, their work explores the nexus of art and commodity. "We question what it means to be an artist in the super-branded cultural climate", say the artists.

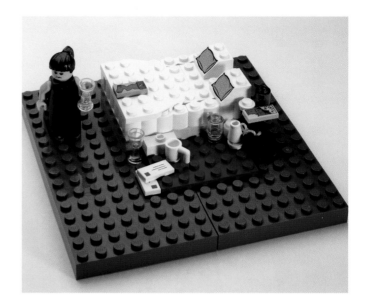

The term engineering thermoplastics is normally given to rigid thermoplastic materials with a degree of mechanical integrity at temperatures around 1,000C. These materials have additives and fillers to enhance their properties, including light stabilisers, antioxidants, plasticisers, lubricants, pigments, flame retardants and metal deactivators. Fillers were used to reinforce the new plastic and improve rigidity as well as increase temperature performance in the short term.

Polyacetals (POM), of which polyformaldehyde is the main example, were developed from 1952 onwards at DuPont. Commercial production began in 1960 under the trade name Delrin. Lightweight and durable engineering plastics, they are used in gearwheels, and bathroom taps. By the 1970s, POM's main use was in the Bic disposable lighter.

Polycarbonate was synthesised by General Electric in America and BASF in Germany. Polycarbonate was commercialised under the trade names Lexan and Makrolan in 1959. Both tough and transparent, environmentally stable and with good electrical properties, polycarbonate is used for applications such as windows and compact discs.

Ethylene-vinyl acetate co-polymers (EVA) were patented by DuPont in 1955. The Elvax range was launched in 1960. EVA is a rubbery type of polymer used for applications ranging from tubing and hose to handle grips and record turn tables. EVA is important in shrink wrap and especially hot melt adhesives.

1960s

More engineering calibre plastics were developed in the 1960s. Carbon fibre composites (CFRCs) were developed at the Royal Aircraft Establishment by Leslie Philips and Willie Watt at Farnborough, in Britain in the mid-1960s. Carbon fibres were developed almost simultaneously in Britain, America and Japan. In Japan, Akio Shindo of the Government Industrial Research Institute in Osaka, used polyacrylonitrile (PAN) as a precursor and this was developed commercially. In America, Rayon was chosen as the precursor and was never developed commercially with any success. CFRCs were initially developed for aerospace applications. CFRCs are combined with resins such as polyester, epoxies and PEEK, to make carbon composite materials. These composites are used in aerospace applications such as military aircraft bodies and in high-end sports applications such as Formula One racing cars, tennis rackets, skis and Olympic level racing canoes and bikes.

The two main applications for the first carbon fibre were the RB211 fan blade and filament wound tubes for centrifuges to separate isotopes of uranium. The RB211 fan blade failed spectacularly following the infamous frozen chicken test.[1] This contributed largely to the bankrupting of Rolls Royce in 1970–1971 and generated much adverse publicity for carbon fibre. The second application was spectacularly successful and was, for a

long time, the largest single application of carbon fibre. However, this information was highly classified at the time, and only a handful of people knew about it.

Courtaulds' commercial advantage, with regard to carbon fibre, was lost due to lack of investment in a new production line; this was crucial due to issues with their existing production line. Toray agreed to build a straight line production facility, won the order and made a commercial success of carbon fibre.

When the Rolls Royce fan blade project failed there was an excess of capacity and manufacturers turned to sports goods to keep the industry alive, such as sporting kayaks, canoes and tennis racquets. For many years in the 1970s and 80s, sales of carbon fibre for sports goods exceeded that for aerospace. It was only after the introduction of CFRP/Nomex honeycomb structures (in order to reduce the weight of the wing flaps in Boeing 757 and 767 civilian aircraft) that carbon fibre sales to the aerospace industry overtook sports goods. Today almost all the secondary structures of civil aircraft are made of carbon fibre/epoxy resin honeycomb-cored constructions, along with some primary structures such as tail fins. Military aircraft such as the AV8B (the US version of the Harrier jump jet) have most of their primary structure, including the wings, made of carbon fibre/epoxy composites. The latest and most ambitious target is a filament wound carbon fibre/epoxy complete fuselage for the latest large Boeing airliner, the Boeing 787 'Dreamliner'. None of this would have been possible without the very successful development of extremely complex epoxy resins to match the demanding needs of aerospace. This success is also a testament to the skill of the manufacturing pre-pregging and filament winding industries which, in very different ways, combine fibre and resin to make successful composites.

Elsewhere, a high-end design-led application of carbon fibre reinforced composites has been in the carbon fibre halogen Lola lamp, designed in 1989 by Italian engineer Alberto Meda and the architect Paolo Rizzatto.

Kevlar was developed by Stephanie Kwolek, at DuPont in 1966, in a continuation of the programme of research into polymer structure begun by Carothers in the 1930s. Kevlar (aramid fibres) are related to the nylons (polyamides) but are much stronger and tougher—their strength is comparable to steel. Kevlar fibres are used for bulletproof vests and protective clothing as well as ropes and aircraft components.

Polyethylene terephthalate (PET), PETP and polybutylene terephthalate (PBT) are engineering polymers that are also used as blends in applications where excellent processing characteristics as well as high strength and rigidity are needed. Oriented blow-moulded drinks containers were launched in 1977 based on PET polymers and other types of polymer such as PBT.

Polysulphones are engineering polymers introduced by ICI, 3M and Union Carbide in 1965. They possess a variety of high value applications, ranging from medical uses in sterilising trays and respirators, to food processing, where they are used in cookware for microwaves and parts for milking machines. Polysulphones have electrical and electronic applications such as switch housings. Polysulphones have many uses in engineering—in car engine components, aerospace and business machine components as well as in composites. Polysulphones were the first successful high temperature thermoplastics.

Polyphenylene oxide (PPO) polymers were introduced by General Electric in 1966. Engineering polymers' applications include coffee pot and washing machine parts, where high temperature and moisture are critical, and also microwave components. PPO was also used to make an electric kettle—although the tea tasted horrible. Acetal copolymer was the first and very successful material used to make a plastic electric kettle. However, the drive for low costs led to the use of polypropylene, but this particular polymer operates very near to its limit in this particular application.

In 1968 General Electric introduced Noryl, a blend of polyphenylene ether (PPO) and polystyrene. PPO is strong, but difficult to form under 200C. PS has low toughness, but is easily formed, and the blend has enhanced not only short term temperature performance between 208C and 100C, but also formability and impact toughness. This material competes with ABS and polycarbonate in its applications.

1970-2000

ICI's polyethersulphone, which launched in 1975, and had outstanding chemical resistance but, crucially, was attacked by synthetic hydraulic fluid used in aircraft. Polyaryletheretherketone (PEEK) was first prepared by ICI in 1977. PEEK was released in very experimental quantities in the mid-1980s and the material could withstand the hydraulic fluids but its very high price and limited availability has impeded its uptake by the aerospace industry. It is used for high end engineering applications as a resin to make high-value composite materials for use in aerospace components. PEEK's current usage is negligible compared with carbon fibre/epoxy composites. This reflects the fact that existing materials used in aerospace applications have undergone exhaustive testing backed by huge investment. Any new material has to undergo extensive testing, and the company who introduces it is forced to pay all the costs of these tests, effectively ruling out the new material.

The 1970s also saw more engineering plastics developed: Phillips' polyphenylenesulphide (PPS) and ICI's polyarylethersulphone (PES). Union Carbide introduced polyphenylsulphone and polyarylethersulphone and GE

BELOW: Metal-on-plastic hip replacement was developed in the 1960s by Sir John Charnley at the Wrightington Hospital near Wigan. The Charnley Hip is expected to last upwards of 12 to 15 years, but is less effective in younger patients where, with perpetual use, the weakest point of the prosthetic hip wears away. The accumulation of plastic dust can cause rejection by the body which in turn undermines and loosens the hip replacement. This rejection can sometimes seriously compromise the surgeon's ability to repeat the operation.

OPPOSITE: Crash test dummy, 2008. Like a fashion mannequin, the dummy looks human, but where a mannequin's beauty is skin-deep, the dummy is fabricated from high-tech instrumentation and state of the art plastic. The crash test dummy relays crash information to sensitive computers via a highly effective series of electrical outputs. Dummies have been dropped out of airplanes, strapped into crashing helicopters, and shot from cannons.

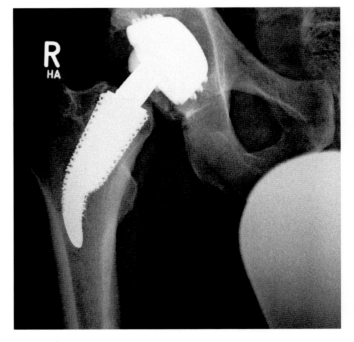

introduced polyetherimide (PEI). Blended engineering polymers produced were Bayer AG's polycarbonate/ABS, and GE Europe's polycarbonate/polyester which was used in car bumpers.

Ultra high molecular weight polyethylene (UHMWPE) was developed in the 1980s, and one application has been in artificial hip joints, although the results have not been totally successful. Later, in 1983, ICI and Bayer launched PEEK, PPS (polyphenylene sulphide), and PES (polyether sulphone) as a group of engineering plastics, with enhanced and dependable properties.

The 1990s was the era in which the recycling of plastics began to be an issue. Humble first steps to combat the global usage of plastics included the manufacture of flower pots made from recycled polypropylene by Cookson Plastics. By the end of the 1990s a range of laminates made of recycled plastics were on the market, notably the range designed and made by Smile Plastics. The company has paved the way for other recycled plastic goods in today's market.

In 2005 NASA developed a polythene-based material RFX1 for use in space craft. RFX1 is described as possessing three times the tensile strength of aluminium, and is 2.6 times lighter. RFX1 can be made into a fabric. It can also be moulded into the shape required and it is thought that RFX1 may act as an effective radiation shield, although testing is still underway.

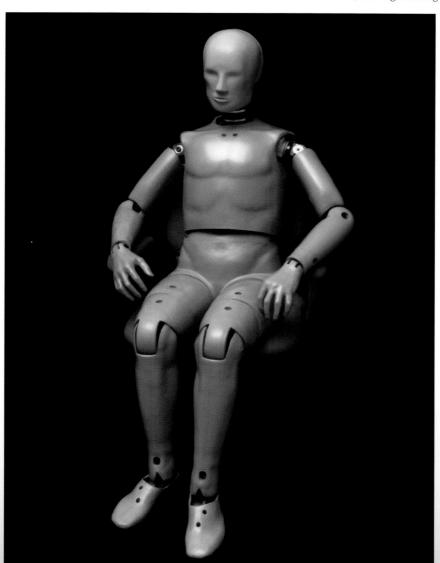

1. The frozen chicken test involves throwing the birds into the rotating blades in order to simulate the effects of birds flying into the engine while the plane is in flight. The blades must be able to withstand this action and keep the plane in flight, for the test to be successful.

FORM IN
PLASTIC

Early plastics, such as Celluloid and casein, are found decorated with classic Victorian ornate motifs. Later, with the advent of Art Nouveau in the 1880s, decoration on domestic ornamental items reflects this influence, with tendril design, female figures decorating the lids and sides of boxes, and general ornamental motifs being moulded into the forms. In Paris, Eduard Fornells Marco, produced a range of decorative cosmetic boxes, reflecting a mixture of earlier Art Nouveau influences and some of the geometric flavour common in the Art Deco style. Marco used cellulose acetate and later urea formaldehyde as the material from which to make his highly desirable ornamental domestic wares.

Art Deco was perhaps the design form which is most memorable in early plastics. With an array of new plastics to choose from, including cellulosics, casein, phenolics, cast phenolics and urea formaldehyde, the Art Deco influence could reveal itself in a variety of ways. This included the use of Assyrian motifs, influenced by the excavations at Nineveh in ancient Assyria (modern Iraq). British designer, Albert Henry 'Woody' Woodfull, showed this Assyrian characteristic in his design of Elo Ware boxes in 1936. Produced by Birkby's, the box lids show hunting scenes quite clearly suggesting the wall reliefs of ancient Assyrian Nineveh. The ancient civilisations were also to influence form in buildings, such as the Chrysler building in New York, and small-scale domestic items, such as candlesticks and ashtrays in Britain and America. Woodfull also designed scenes of Grecian warriors on the lid of a cigarette box for the Ardath Tobacco Company, manufactured by Streetly Manufacturing, in 1935.

Howard Carter's excavations of the tomb of Tutankhamen, in Egypt from 1922, were to have a very strong Egyptianising influence on the Art Deco movement. Results of this were visible architecturally, but also on a smaller scale in casein pendants, designed using Egyptian inspiration, portraying faces in profile, or reflecting Egyptian motifs such as the lotus flower, as well as designed in dramatic, clean, geometrical lines.

Reco Capey, RSA, was an influential, but rather forgotten, designer who designed a series of decorative cosmetic boxes in the 1930s for Yardley's.

By the 1930s, Art Deco design was reflected in plastic items and those who manufactured plastic goods made efforts to make them look attractive and reflect modern taste. The Art Deco influence was so strong that it was to linger on as late as 1948, with the production of the Carvacraft series of cast phenolic desk accessories, made in imitation jade and amber and reflecting strong Art Deco form with columned and stepped designs. Carvacraft was produced by the John Dickinson Company in Britain and is very collectible today.

152

In America the streamlined, modernist movement became current and was reflected in Art Deco in Europe. Streamlined design suited the production of thermosetting plastics, such as Bakelite and urea formaldehyde, which had to be compression-moulded. The simpler the lines of the mould, the easier the production process became. Credit for this influential line of high-end design products must lie with the Bakelite Corporation and Allan Brown, who set the standard for good design in plastics at an early stage in the 1920s.

Design classics include Raymond Loewy's Bakelite Purma special camera for Thomas de la Rue, 1934; Walter Teague's Brownie camera for Kodak; Harold van Doren's designs for the radio cabinet for Air King Products Company, 1933, and the Sentinel scales for the Toledo Scale Company, 1935, both made of one-piece Plaskon urea formaldehyde. Other classics produced were American designer, WB Petzold's, phenolic (Bakelite) Calendaire.

Using a different plastic, Paul T Frankl designed a Celluloid brush and comb set, inspired by the, "so-called modernistic art", according to the Celluloid Corporation who had commissioned him. Donald Deskey was to make innovative and influential use of plastic laminates in Art Deco interiors, using characteristically geometric lines and an austere style according to Jeffery Meikle, an eminent historian of American plastics. Meikle has made a detailed study of this new mood in American plastics design of the 1930s. In the book *Form and Re-form*, dedicated to contemporary design, Frankl referred to plastics as, "Material Nova... expressive of our own age." In 1940, the American journal, *Fortune*, reviewed the plastics industry, and referred to a new continent of plastics, Synthetica, which they represented as a map with the countries named after various plastics.

OPPOSITE: Brownie camera with geometric styling by American designer Walter Dorwin Teague, circa 1930, with enamelled front and leatherette covered sides. Originally marketed by George Eastman as an inexpensive, mass-market camera, the Brownie made photography accessible to the masses. It was cheap and extremely simple to use, even for children. Designed by Frank Brownell, the Brownie was literally a cardboard box with a wooden end. Eastman named the camera after characters popularised by the Canadian children's author, Palmer Cox, illustrations of which feature on the packaging for the camera. Manufactured by Eastman Kodak Company, Rochester, New York. The Baby Brownie introduced in 1934 had a Bakelite body. Courtesy of Science and Society.

STREAMLINED DESIGN SUITED THE PRODUCTION OF THERMOSETTING PLASTICS, SUCH AS BAKELITE AND UREA FORMALDEHYDE, WHICH HAD TO BE COMPRESSION-MOULDED

DESIGN
1940-PRESENT

BELOW: The classic Panton Chair's simple form is a big part of its irresistible charm. Designed in 1968, it epitomises the era's approach to furniture design, which was all about experimentation—new shapes, new colours and, most importantly, new materials, especially plastics. The Chair was originally known as the S Chair.

OPPOSITE TOP: Arne Jacobsen's modernist classic, the Egg, combines modernist ideals with Jacobsen's Scandinavian love of naturalism. Designed for the Royal SAS Hotel, Copenhagen, the highly sculptured Egg Chair is the result of Jacobsen's quest for a curved fluid form that was lightweight, required minimum padding, and was still comfortable. A few limited edition Egg couches were also produced.

OPPOSITE BOTTOM: Early 1960s Ericafon by Ericsson. Developments in plastics allowed Ericsson to create the first one-piece phone. Originally designed in 1957, the sleek Swedish design was also known as the Cobra phone.

By the late 1940s, new design influences were coming into play, as well as a whole range of new plastics. Most were thermoplastic, so could be blow-moulded, vacuum-moulded, and rotational-moulded, as well as made by more conventional moulding techniques, such as injection moulding. Resin transfer moulding (RTM) was developed for moulding composite materials. The main applications of RTM have been in yachts and sports cars. Lotus developed vacuum assisted RTM and were world leaders in this field. Furniture design was a key area where form was liberated, leading to a range of chairs never before possible with conventional materials. Notable was Charles Eames' GRP stackable chair of 1948, nicknamed La Chaise.

In 1949, the furniture company, Hille, commissioned British designer Robin Day to design furniture for mass-production. Over the next 44 years he created more than 150 designs for domestic and office furniture and public seating.

The Festival of Britain, 1951, was intended to celebrate the renaissance in British design. Form became more rounded and new designers arrived, producing a range of plastics domestic ware used, not only for picnic sets, but in the home and for air travel. Gaby Schreiber was a leading light in plastics design at this time. Of Austrian descent, Schreiber came to Britain where she applied Bauhaus principles to guide her design ethos. She designed plastics cutlery for the forces, and following the Second World War she designed kitchen and household equipment for Runcolite Ltd.. Plastics design historian and writer Sylvia Katz has likened "Her elegant colander of 1948 [as] equal to the best contemporary Italian design." Schreiber gained the title of the "The Plastic Queen of England" when she designed a cup for use on aircraft.

GRP had enormous influence on car design. The Chevrolet Corvette with glass reinforced plastic body was produced by the American Company, General Motors in 1953. The British Reliant Regal 111, with GRP body, was manufactured in 1956.

1960s

In 1961 Ronald E Brookes designed the Fiesta Range. This tableware was made of melamine—a tough, temperature resistant plastic and was manufactured by Brookes & Adams. In 1968 David Harmon-Powell designed the Nova tableware range for Ekco Plastics Ltd..

The key area where plastics influenced design was in that of chair design. At the end of the 1950s Arne Jacobsen had produced his Egg and Swan chairs (1958). By 1961 Marco Zanuso's one-piece child's stackable polypropylene chair had become popular, as was Saarinen's Tulip Chair collection. In 1963, Robin Day designed the polypropylene stacking chair for Hille, which became one of the best-selling chairs of all time. Verner Panton's stackable

BELOW: Panton Plexiglas Chair, armchair with high back form 1961.

OPPOSITE: Eero Aarnio's Ball Chair, 1966, was sometimes called the Globe Chair. The design is a simple geometric form—literally a ball—fixed at one point. Described as a "room within a room", the Chair turns on its own axis, giving the user a variable view of the world.

Panton Chair was designed in 1967 for Vitra, and became a classic of design. Originally made in Luran-S, then polyurethane foam, then polystyrol, the Panton Chair is now made in polypropylene.

Finnish designer, Eero Aarnio designed his Ball or Globe Chair in 1966, with a fibreglass shell and a foam cushioned interior. Described as "a room within a room", it epitomises the 1960s spirit of fun furniture and became a visible presence in its own right in the 1960s TV series of *The Prisoner*.

The Plia folding and stacking Chair, made of Perspex and steel, was designed in 1969 by Giancarlo Piretti. It became a classic design; eventually produced in a toughened version of cellulose acetate.

On the art front, American Claes Oldenburg created a series of soft PVC sculptures in the 1960s, including a soft bathtub.

Irish born conceptual artist Les Levine specialised in disposable art and environmental places and became known for wearing a white 'vinyl' suit. In 1969 *Life* magazine named him "Plastic Man". Levine created a series of disposable plastic art installations, including *Disposable Wall*, 1968, made from transparent polystyrene, and *Windows* made of polyester Mylar sheet. His concept of environmental places culminated with *Star Garden*, installed at the Museum of Modern Art in New York in 1967, and made of seven foot high reflective clear acrylic panels containing large half bubbles. "The visitor was invited to walk between instead of around these bubbles. The process was supposed to induce 'giddiness' and 'weightlessness', which in turn would make the viewer feel like a star in outer space."[1]

Some of the most inspirational and visionary uses of plastics have been proposed by architects. However, most plastic houses— from imagined giant inflatable cities, to Monsanto's 1954 House of the Future—have remained as prototypes or firmly on the drawing board. Clearly influenced by the space race, Finnish architect, Matti Suuronen, designed the Futuro House, to take advantage of plastics' lightweight and modern aesthetic. The GRP Futuro House, designed in 1968, was one of the few Houses of the Future to make it into production, and to have lasting cultural impact, with the Futuro brochure of the late 1960s claiming, "Futuro represents the modern, comfortable way of housing—practical coziness. Futuro is the dwelling of future."

1970s

While on the large scale, the inflatable Fuji Group Pavilion PVC building, was designed for the 1970 Expo exhibition, in the laboratory significant developments were occurring with the advent of conductive polymers. Polyacetylene (also known as polyethyne) was one of the first known examples of a conductive organic polymer and Alan J Heeger, Alan G MacDiarmid and Hideki Shirakawa were awarded the 2000 Nobel Prize in Chemistry for their work on this.

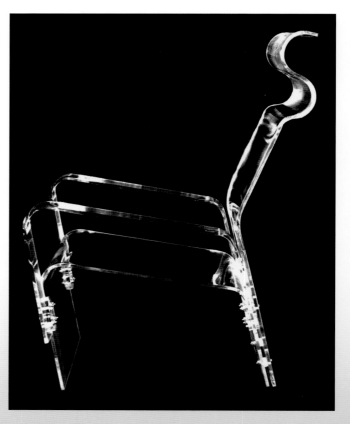

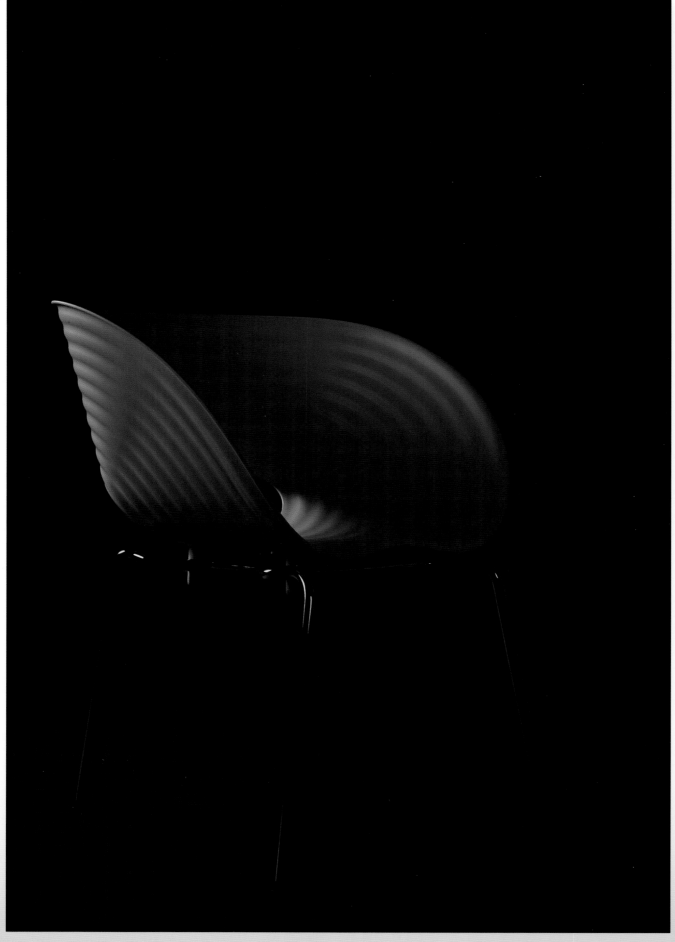

1980s

The extraordinary, organically formed Dalila Chair, made in rigid polyurethane foam, was designed by Gaetano Pesce for Cassina, Italy in 1980.

Israeli-born iconoclastic designer, Ron Arad, has always been innovative and adventurous with both his use of plastics and their form. Arad has designed a series of interesting plastic furniture, including his 1983 Transformer furniture, made of an inflatable PVC envelope containing expanded polystyrene beads. Famous for his flexible PVC Bookworm, shelving system, Arad also designed the Tom Vac Chair in 1997. Made of corrugated acrylic, the Tom Vac Chair is light, stackable and very easy to produce. It became very successful and is still produced in the thousands. Perhaps the height of Arad's daring was the display of a range of his plastic furniture, running in a line down the centre of the London Victoria & Albert Museum's Medieval Gallery in his 2000 retrospective exhibition, *Before and After Now.*

The 1980s were the decade where scientists were exploring the electronic and magnetic properties of polymers. Light Emitting Polymers, such as polyphenylene vinylene, polyaniline and polypyridine, were discovered first at the Cavendish laboratory at the University of Cambridge, in 1989, by a team led by Professor Sir Richard Friend. They are used in Organic Light Emitting Diodes (OLEDs), which have been developed by Cambridge Display Technologies.

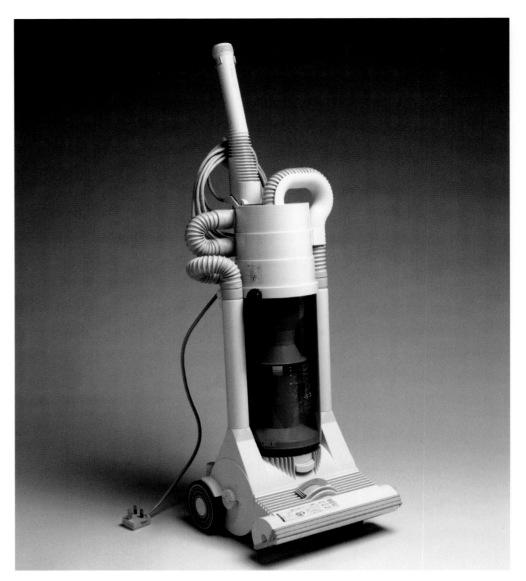

OPPOSITE: Dyson bagless vacuum
cleaner, the first ever vacuum
cleaner created by James Dyson.
The distinctive Cyclone feature
allows continuous suction.
Centrifugal force separates dirt
and dust from the air, which is
then collected in a clear bin.
As there is nothing to block
the airflow, the system does
not clog up or lose suction.
Courtesy Science and Society.

BOTTOM: The roof of the
Millennium Dome, London, is a
huge cable net, 320 metres in
diameter, clad in 80,000 square
metres of fabric. The fabric is
made from thin fibres of glass
woven into cloth and dipped ten
times into liquid Teflon, to form
a protective coat. It is just 1
millimetre thick yet each panel
weighs more than a ton. It is an
innovative feat of engineering
by Buro Happold, yet simple in
concept, and was the recipient
of the prestigious MacRobert
Award, 1999.

1990s/2000s

James Dyson, the British industrial designer, produced his now
legendary vacuum cleaner in 1991. In 1993, Alessi produced their
first all plastic product, the Alessi Gino Zucchino sugar pourer,
designed by Guido Venturini. The LotusSport bicycle, made of
carbon fibre was created (ridden to success by Chris Boardman
in the 1992 Olympics) and the Smart car was introduced in 1994,
with lightweight flexible integrally coloured polycarbonate panels.

The amorphous free-standing Zanussi Oz fridge was
launched in 1998, with insulation and outer-skins made in one
process from polyurethane foam. Although the Oz fridge was
discontinued, its innovative design made it an immediately iconic
object, which boosted Zanussi's public image.

In 2001 Jonathan Ive designed the now iconic iPod for
Apple. This followed the pattern of the successful, simple style
guidelines used in the iMac and the iBook. The Millennium Dome
roof was built in 2000 using Teflon coated glass fibre fabric.
Originally contractors were going to use PVC, but there were
protests from some environmentalists.

In 2005 Herman Miller produced the Mirra Chair. This was
designed to be taken apart and to be 96 per cent recyclable.

The iconic postmodern French designer, Philippe Starck
designed the Louis Ghost Chair for Kartell. This was introduced
in 2002. It is an ironic take on a classic Louis XVI Chair design—a
copy of a late eighteenth century, French Neoclassic chair,
circa 1770, but made in transparent polycarbonate. Starck has
commented: "I am a little specialist of high-technology, perhaps
plastic, because I love plastic. First for ecological reasons,
because the more you use plastic in an intelligent and ethical
way, the less often you kill animals to have the leather, the less
often you kill trees to have wood." By 2006 Starck had produced
his Lux range of disposable plastic champagne flutes, dockable
into the Lux plates, with gold and/or silver plastic cutlery.
Presumably this is a further piece of irony and humour on the
designer's part. One can only think of a comparison with the
Tupperware champagne goblets.

1. Time magazine, 5 May, 1967.

NEW
PLASTICS

The Loremo concept car (Low resistance mobile) combines traditional materials such as steel with thermoplastics to make a light, energy efficient structure.

The non-load-bearing, self-supporting, thermoplastic body panels mould to the linear cell structure and help the Loremo to achieve its aerodynamic shape. This material has a number of advantages: it is lightweight, weatherproof, scratch-resistant and economical.

New plastics are being developed in a variety of fields—in aerospace, medicine, everyday living, textiles, electronics and engineering. The world of so-called smart materials and plastics are constantly under development. Smart plastics respond to external stimuli in their environment—heat, light, magnetic fields, electricity or stress. There is a whole new range of thermochromic plastic materials being produced. Thermochromic plastics respond to heat by changing colour; conduct electricity or magnetism; emanate light in the form of light emitting diodes and change their shape in response to external stresses. Today, we have piezoelectric and pyroelectric polymers, used for particular applications, ranging from loud speakers to heat sensors. Polymers which are capable of changing shape may be used in the shape-changing planes of the future. Phase-changing polymers have been developed that under pressure or impact change from a viscous to a solid state and are finding applications in protective clothing, for example in down-hill skiing suits.

Techno-textiles are being researched and developed, and are being used in high fashion, the military, sports and experimental fashion. These are often synthetic plastic fibres, which are then treated using various processes to produce constructed textiles. Techno-textiles may be coated with metals and heat-moulded, formed in a variety of shapes, integrated with optical fibres to make light emitting fabrics, or woven together with conductive fibres to fulfil packaging or medical applications.

In medicine, plastics are used to coat time-delivery drugs, such as Deprovera, the female contraceptive. Polymer encapsulated drugs are being developed to deliver gene therapies. Plastic blood—the goal of many a medical polymer scientist—has been developed using the complex polymer tetraphenolporphyrin-cored hyperbranched polyglycidol. Plastic blood is designed to be used in the field in emergencies. More recent medical advances include germ-killing plastics, based on polystyrene bonded to chlorine atoms, which have recently been launched in a range of filters to clean dirty water. In 2007 a plastic very similar to the membranes that surround our body cells has been developed called poly(ethylene oxide)-co-poly(butylene oxide) (PEO-PBO). One day this might be used for gene therapy.

Bioengineering has been a significant area for the use of and developments in plastic materials—acrylic corneas, polyester for artificial veins; nylon for sutures; silicone rubbers for artificial ears and noses; silicone for artificial implants; polythene for cups in artificial hip joints. Research is ongoing into the use of ultra high molecular weight polyethene for use in hip joints.

Plastics have played an important role in dental applications—from the first Vulcanite dentures, to the exploding Celluloid dentures and the modern, acrylic dentures. *Gutta percha* played an important role as an early dental filling material; new plastics that cure under blue light are now heavily in use. The near future portends custom made teeth that will be computer-designed and made.

In electronics, light emitting diodes have been made of a polymer called polyphenylene vinylene. The first plastic chips to replace silicon chips now exist. Bendy elastic screens, which have readable text, are hitting the market so instead of reading books on the train, commuters will be able to read a rollable screen. Plastic solar cells have been produced and their performance is being improved.

Aerospace has been a leader in the development of new plastics whether it be as composites for high-tech applications such as aircraft wings and bodies, or for self-healing structures. Shape memory plastics, in addition to composite and electronic plastics, are being used in shape changing planes to optimise flight conditions and speed.

BIOMIMETICS

Smart design is now an important new field in materials science. Designers and materials scientists are looking to nature for inspiration, a field called Biomimetics. They have examined the feet of the gecko that adheres to surfaces, and transferred this principle into polymer-based "gecko" gloves or shoes that can stick to vertical surfaces. Others have looked for inspiration to the lotus flower, which always remains clean due to the array of tiny hairs on its surface, and this concept has been applied to the field of self-cleaning fabrics. Teflon-coated fabrics are now on the market, designed to repel stains. As self-repairing fabrics are another area under development—there may be a future where clothes neither need to be mended or laundered.

Building on the continuing success of GORE-TEX, engineered fibres are an important area of applied polymer science. Polyester fibres in particular have been modified to meet demanding expectations by sports clothing wearers. Developed for sport, these new fibres have been transferred into the leisure market—a multi-million dollar industry.

The plastic fibres used in high-tech applications by companies such as DuPont are engineered to contain channels, which are able to cool the wearer and wick moisture away from the body. Other fibres contain so-called themocules—small molecules which adapt to the heat and the cold, keeping the wearer comfortable at all times.

THE FUTURE OF SPORT

Olympic sports suits are now designed using polymeric fabrics that integrate biomimetic principles of design—that is imitate nature's best designs. These include the neoprene shark swimming suit, worn by gold medal winner Ian Thorpe, at the 2000 Sydney Olympics. The shark design was developed by a

Scientific advances are now closing the gap between real and prosthetic limbs. It is now possible to create connections between the brain and prosthesis, allowing the appropriate nerve endings to react when the brain sends out signals. Plastics play a key role in the manufacture of prosthetics due to their lightness and versatility. Courtesy Getty Images.

shark specialist, from London's Natural History Museum, who worked with Adidas, a leading company working in high-tech sport clothing. Lycra running suits have also been designed which integrate specialised pressure panels into the thighs to support the athletes while running. High-tech running shoes such as the Predator, worn by footballer David Beckham, have been designed that imitate the skin of a shark. The company, Nike, is at the forefront of this type of research and has developed specialised running shoes for men and women. Each running shoe uses a variety of polymers in its make up.

POLYMER DEVELOPMENT

Other polymers have been developed which change from liquid to solid on impact and are being used in protective clothing for sports, such as downhill skiing, and are becoming increasingly popular as they are lighter and less bulky than conventional protective clothing.

Cheap, home-based methods of plastics production are being developed. The idea is called "home fabrication": objects can be designed on a home computer, the pattern is then sent to the three-dimensional printer which produces the item. Prototypes of such home-based machines are the American Fab@Home printer, and the British Rep Rap printer.

BELOW: Stacked piles of household plastic waste to be recycled. Americans use 2.5 million plastic bottles every hour. The urgency to recycle in order to save the environment has never been so prevalent.

OPPOSITE: Polyethylene terephthalate (PET) bottles are normally made from recycled bottles such as this.

PLASTICS RECYCLING

The recycling of plastic, and the effect of plastic on the environment, is becoming ever more important.

In 2007 Britain generated nearly three million tons of plastics waste and it is estimated that only seven per cent of this was recycled. This figure is improving following new European Union legislation on landfill and packaging waste, as well as improved efforts by local authorities to increase recycling, the result being that, in 2007, five times as many plastic bottles were recycled as in 2002. This trend is expected to continue.

As the availability of cheap oil looks uncertain, making new plastics out of waste is not only more environmentally-friendly, but could also become the cheapest option. As well as conserving resources, recycling plastic uses less energy than making plastic from new raw materials. To produce high-quality plastic from recycling, it helps if recyclers can melt each plastic down separately. This is difficult when products contain many different materials, or when plastics are reinforced with other fibres for strength. The greenest design often means simple materials and simple construction.

New composite materials are being developed that can be melted (are thermoplastic) instead of thermosetting. These are still tough but are made from a single plastic, polypropylene, reinforced with stretched polypropylene fibres.

Most of our plastics waste ends up as bin bags, park benches and pipes, but some has a more glamorous second life. Rubber soles can make artificial grass, cushioning inner foam from running shoes becomes a tennis court and the upper synthetic fabric can be ground into padding for wooden basketball floors. Old carrier bags have been turned into designer jewellery. From these examples it is clear that recycling plastics does not compromise design quality.

Plastics waste at Chongqing,
China. A scavenger picks up
plastic bags at an open dump
on April 2, 2008. The Chinese
government has announced
a nationwide ban on stores
distributing free ultra-thin
plastic bags from 1 June, 2008.
The new rule demands retailers
must clearly indicate the price
of their plastic bags and charge
customers for them.
The Chinese use up to three
billion plastic bags a day,
equivalent to about five million
tons of crude oil, according to
reports. Photograph courtesy of
Getty Images.

SUSTAINABLE PLASTICS

Biopolymers, which are made from natural materials such as plants, are being researched and in production. Examples include spider silk. The aim for this work is to reproduce a synthetic form of the spiders' dragline silk, which is 50 times stronger, weight for weight, than steel.

The first biopolymer, developed by ICI in the 1970s, was called Biopol. It was made by feeding plant sugars to bacteria, and designed to be biodegradable. The problem was that it was initially used to make bottles. After consideration it became clear that, in terms of this application, it was more ecologically-sound to simply reuse existing bottles. Biopol is now used for applications such as yogurt pot tops, which are less easily reusable.

Plastics are now being grown from plants such as corn and sugar cane. This occurs in a variety of ways—whether by growing bacteria on the plant or by a form of genetic splicing. Plastics produced in this way include polylactic acid, and polyhydroxyalkanoate (PHA); both are biodegradable. However, a great amount of energy has to be put into extracting the plastics from their plants and so, for the moment, the energy equations do not quite tally. Polylactic acid (PLA), is a plastic that comes from chemicals found in corn and is used for applications such as mobile phone casings and carpet.

One of the biggest users of plant-based plastics has been the car industry. As well as using plastics made from plants, car designers are using plant fibres to strengthen plastic, replacing conventional carbon fibre or glass reinforcement. Plastics reinforced with plant fibres are much lighter than traditional composites, so the cars are much more energy-efficient to drive. An example is the Toyota iUnit Concept Car, designed in Japan. The car body is made of tough kenaf plant fibres held together by lignin, a natural polymer found in wood.

Scientists are working to find new sources of plastic that are sustainable for the future. We currently make almost all of our plastics from oil, gas and coal, which are not renewable. Plastics from plants are not an ideal solution— they still require land to grow them and energy to process them—but they could ease our reliance on oil. Some of these plastics have the added bonus that they will degrade into compost at the end of their life, completing the cycle found in the natural world.

BELOW: The Brelli is the first environmentally responsible umbrella made from 100 per cent biodegradable plastic with bamboo struts and handle. Brainchild of Pam Zonsuis, a New York based designer, its efficient design uses biopolymers which decompose completely at the end of its life. Photograph courtesy of Brelli.

FOLLOWING PAGES: Urn for keeping placenta in powder (LEFT) and casket for burying placenta (RIGHT), Benjamin Graindorge, 2008. First exhibited in Duende Collective's exhibition, La part des Anges' (Angels' Share), the show explored our earliest eating habits, including pre-natal intra uterine links via the placenta, and post-natal links via breast feeding. Made from pink gold and sunflower bio plastic, respectively, demonstrating alternative uses of ecologically sound plastics.

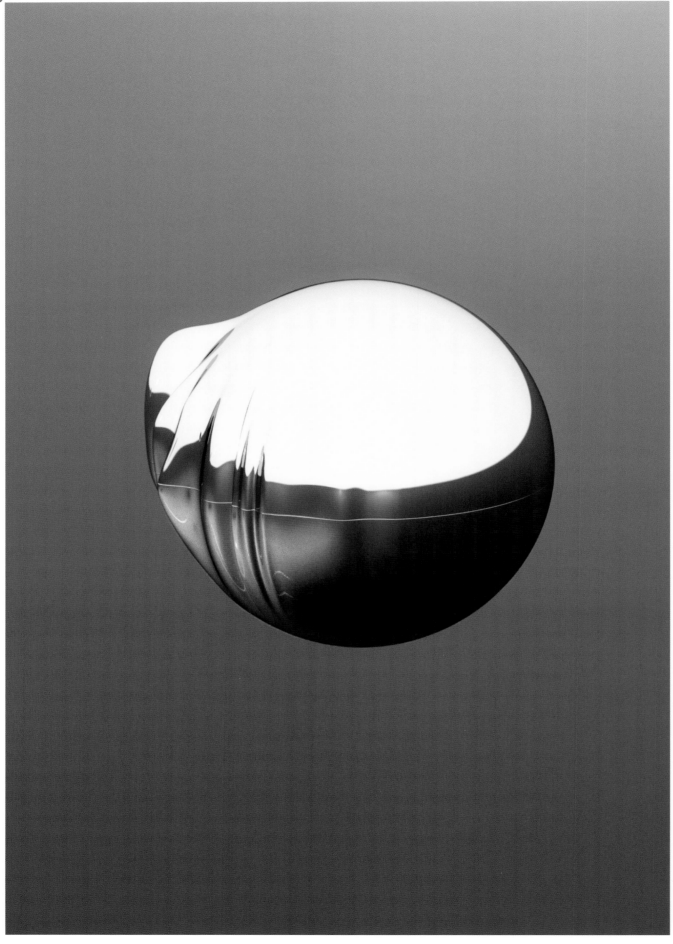

FANTASTIC
PLASTIC?

In 2007 the world produced 230 million tons of plastics; 60 million tons of this was polythene. This is a massive increase from the five million tons of plastics globally consumed in the 1950s. Plastics are increasingly likely to be engineered for specific purposes. The fashion industry has adopted these new materials with enthusiasm and is looking more and more at how both high-tech materials and production processes could be adapted to the needs of fashion and clothing. Certain plastics will become increasingly adaptable, whether in form, colour or composition. We might be able to wear clothing that changes shape and colour according to our mood, and already aromatherapy is being integrated into fabrics to enhance our mood.

The medical industry is increasingly looking for plastics which are responsive to the wearer—one can envisage a future where we wear a plastic strip on our skin, which monitors our blood pressure and general health. In certain cases such strips may even be used to deliver medicine into our skin. Already plastics encapsulated drugs are being used to deliver drugs inside the body, over a specific timed period.

GREEN DESIGN

Green design is becoming a key mantra for designers. In future plastics products will be designed with their whole lifecycle in mind, from cradle to cradle, so that when they have fulfilled their life in one way they can then be reused, recycled or adapted to fit a new function.

Many scientists remain focused on developing, adapting and combining plastics. Meanwhile, other plastics specialists are thinking about the alternatives. Some are looking for new sources of plastic, hoping to reduce our dependency on oil, with its uncertain future. Others, including product designers, are planning ways to reduce waste and promote a more responsible approach to our plastic world. It is not only in recent times that inventors and advertisers have seen plastics in a futuristic light. As early as 1941, scientists Yarsley and Couzens imagined 'Plastic Man', whom they predicted would live completely cocooned in plastics from birth to death.

FANTASTIC PLASTIC?

There are both positive and negative aspects to the world of plastics, which have been explored in this book. The latest generation of plastics have come a long way from their semi-synthetic beginnings in the mid-nineteenth century. Many are responsive, literally changing shape or colour. Some protect us from impact or disease. Others store energy or conduct electricity.

All of these factors promote the positive aspects of plastic. However, over 150 years of production and consumption has led to a mountain of plastic waste. New laws will discourage

OPPOSITE: Artificial plant by Frank Tjepkema for Droog, an innovative design enterprise based in Amsterdam. This unapologetically fake rubber plant makes no attempt to conceal its artifice. "Why should artificial plants look like the real thing when the real thing looks really real?" asks Tjepkema. Photograph by Ron van Keulen.

BOTTOM: The X-Finger® is the world's first active-function artificial finger. Created by Didrick Medical Inc., the device is designed to allow users to bend and flex an artificial finger in a realistic way. Covered with a silicone finger sheath, it almost looks like the real thing.

dependency on landfill, so there will be a need to look at all the ways plastics may be reused, recycled or biodegrade. In future it may be necessary to excavate and reuse the plastics in landfill or in rubbish bins in the form of new plastics or as fuel. Views of plastics may change. If they become rare or have exceptional properties, they may become more valuable.

Plastic packaging, including the nature of its disposal, is now in the public eye. Food packaging in particular is often complex and multi-layered. Simpler materials solutions may need to be found so that the shelf life of food may be enhanced by packaging but also so that the packaging degrades when thrown away in a swift timescale, not littering the landscape, beaches and waterways and oceans, or filling our landfill for centuries.

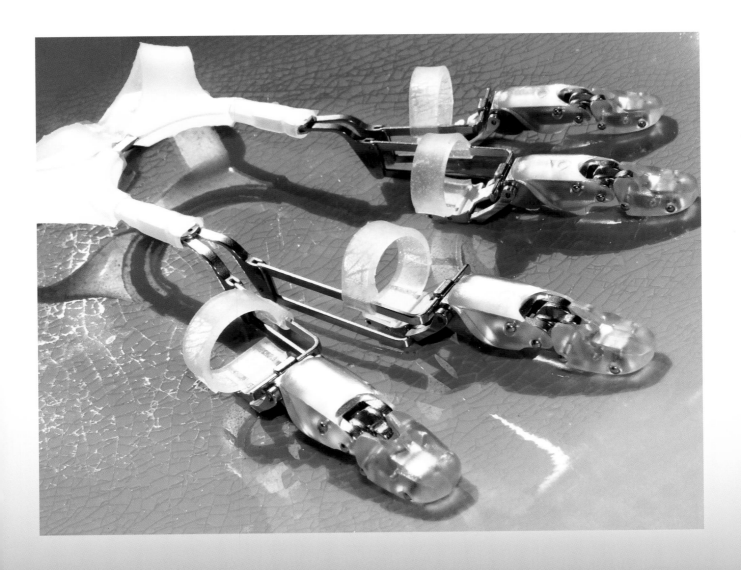

THE FUTURE
WAS
PLASTIC

OPPOSITE: Futuro House, 1968. Finnish architect, Matti Suuronen, designed this UFO shaped dwelling for use as a ski cabin or holiday home. The Futuro House was completely furnished and could accommodate eight people. Made of reinforced plastic, the plan was to mass-produce it, so it would be cheap but the oil crisis in the mid-1970s ended this dream, and only about a hundred Futuro houses were ever built.

When considering the effect of plastics in today's society it is fitting, perhaps, to reflect back to Yarsley and Couzens' futuristic vision of a plastic world: "Brighter and cleaner... free from moth and rust and full of colour... built up of synthetic materials in which man, like a magician, makes what he wants for almost every need." Walt Disney imagined a 1950s atomic spaceship with plastic radiation-blocking shielding. This still remains a dream, although new research may make this dream come true in the relatively near future. Many developments in plastics have delivered real changes to our daily lives: disposable contact lenses and cheap and lightweight plastic kettles, vacuum cleaners, mobile phones and other portable gadgets, as well as comfortable, elasticated clothing and high-tech, high fashion materials and a range of bioengineering implants which improve or may even save the quality of the receptor's life. It would now be hard for those of us living in Europe and America to imagine a life without plastics, as they now play such an integral part in our lifestyle.

IT WOULD NOW BE HARD FOR THOSE OF US LIVING IN EUROPE AND AMERICA TO IMAGINE A LIFE WITHOUT PLASTICS

PLASTICS
SOURCES

SELECTED BOOKS

Battle, D and Lesser, A, *The Best of Bakelite and Other Plastic Jewellery*,
Pennsylvania: Schiffer Publishing Ltd, 1996.
Barthes, R, *Mythologies*, London: Paladin, 1989 (original edition 1959).
Braddock, SE and O'Mahony, M, *Technotextiles: Revolutionary Fabrics for
Fashion and Design*, London: Thames and Hudson, 2002.
Brydson, JA, *Plastics Materials*, Oxford: Butterworth Heinemann, 1989.
Budnitz, P, *I Am Plastic: The Designer Toy Explosion*, New York: Abrams, 2006.
Campos, C (ed), *Plastic*, New York: Collins Design, 2007.
Clarke, AJ, *Tupperware: The Promise of Plastic in 1950s America*,
Washington DC: Smithsonian Institution Press, 1999.
Couzens, EG and Yarsley, VE, *Plastics*, New York: Pelican, 1941; updated edition 1968.
DiNoto, A, *Art Plastic: Designed for Living*, New York: Abbeville, 1984.
Dormer. P. *The meanings of modern design*, London: Thames and Hudson, 1991.
Du Bois, JH, *Plastics History* USA, Boston: Cahners Books, 1972.
Ettienger, R, *Twentieth Century Plastic Jewellery*, Pennsylvania:
Schiffer Publishing Ltd, 2007.
Fenichell, S. *Plastic: The Making of a Synthetic Century*, New York:
Harperbusiness, 1996.
Friedel, R, *Pioneer Plastic: The Making and Selling of Celluloid*, Wisconsin
and London: University of Wisconsin Press, 1983.
Gloag, J, *Plastics and Industrial Design*, London: George Allen Unwin Press, 1945.
Hancock, T, *Personal Narrative of the Origin and Progress of the Caoutchouc or India
Rubber Manufacture in England*, London: Longman, 1857.
Handley, S, *Nylon: The Story of a Fashion Revolution*, Baltimore:
Johns Hopkins University Press, 1999.
Hard, AH, *The Romance of Rayon*, Manchester: Whittaker & Robinson, 1933.
Imhoff, D, *Paper or Plastic: Searching for Solutions to an Overpackaged World*,
San Francisco: Sierra Club Books, 2005.
Katz, S, *Plastics: Design and Materials*, London: Studio Vista, 1978.
Katz, S, *Classic Plastics*, London: Thames & Hudson, 1984.
Kaufman, M, *The First Century of Plastics—Celluloid and its Sequel*, London:
The Plastics and Rubber Institute, 1963 (reprinted 1980).
Loadman, J, *Tears of the Tree*, Oxford: Oxford University Press, 2005.
Meikle, JL, *American Plastic*, New Brunswick, New Jersey:
Rutgers University Press, 1995.
Morris, PJT, *Polymer Pioneers*, Philadelphia: Beckmann Center for the
History of Chemistry, 1990.
Mossman, ST and Morris, PJT (ed), *The Development of Plastics*, Cambridge:
The Royal Society of Chemistry, 1994.
Mossman, ST (ed), *Early Plastics: Perspectives 1850–1950*, London:
Leicester University Press, 1997 (Paperback edition, Continuum Press, 2000).
Mumford, J, *The Story of Bakelite*, 1924.
Pascale, A and Cernia, F, *Gli anni di Plastica*, Milan: Electra Editrice, 1983.
Phoenix, W, *Plastic Culture: How Japanese Toys Conquered the World*, Tokyo:
Kodansha International Ltd, 2006.
Quye, A and Williamson, C, *Plastics Collecting and Conserving*,
Edinburgh: NMS Publishing Ltd, 1999.
Redhead, D, *Products of Our Time*, Basel: Birkhauser, 2000.
Shashoua, Y, *Conservation of Plastics*, London: Elsevier Science and Technology, 2008.
Sparke, P (ed), *The Plastics Age*, London: Victoria & Albert Museum, 1990.
Waugh, E, *The Ordeal of Gilbert Pinfold*, Harmondsworth: Penguin,
1991 (original edition 1957).
Woodham, JM, *Twentieth Century Design*, Oxford: Oxford University Press, 1997.

USEFUL ADDRESSES

British Plastics Federation
Bath Place, Rivington Street,
London EC2A 3DR, UK.
+44 (0) 207 457 5000.
www.bpf.co.uk

Institute of Materials
Materials Information Service
1 Carlton House Terrace,
London, SW1Y 5DB, UK.
+44 (0) 207 839 4071
www.iom3.org

Plastics Historical Society
c/o The Institute of Materials
1 Carlton House Terrace,
London, SW1Y 5DB, UK.
www.platiquarian.com

Science Museum
Exhibition Road, South Kensington,
London, SW7 2DD, UK.
www.sciencemuseum.org.uk

Smithers Rapra Technology Ltd
Shawbury, Shrewsbury,
Shropshire, SY4 4NR, UK.
www.rapra.net

WEBSITES

Eero Aarnio
www.eero-aarnio.com

The Bakelite Emporium
www.bakeliteman.com

The Bois Durci Information Centre
www.mernick.co.uk

The Brellie
www.thebrelli.com

Ian Cook
www.popbangcolour.com

Patrick Coyle
www.re-title.com/artists/patrick-coyle.asp

Tom Dixon
www.tomdixon.net

Dezeen
www.dezeen.com

Droog Design
www.droogdesign.nl

DuPont
www.dupont.com

Icon Eye
www.iconeye.com

John Cake and Darren Neave
www.littleartist.co.uk

Miwa Koizumi
miwa.metm.org

The Materials Library
www.materialslibrary.org.uk

The Plastics Historical Society
www.plastiquarian.com

The Plastics Museum
www.plasticsmuseum.org

Plastics Network
www.plasticsnetwork.org

Plastics Resource
www.plasticsresource.com

ACKNOWLEDGEMENTS

I want to thank the following people for their contributions in a variety of ways to this book. Firstly, my colleagues on the *Plasticity—100 years of making plastics* exhibition at the Science Museum, Alison Conboy and Helen Peavitt. My thanks also to Norman Waterman, Derek Mossman and Ralph Kay for their useful comments; to friends and colleagues from the Plastics Historical Society, for their informative and congenial company over the years, and finally to Robert Bud who started me on the plastics road.

Susan Mossman
June 2008

A big thanks to everybody who helped on the book, especially Julia Trudeau Rivest for her continual patience, perseverance and stunning, considerate design. Also thank you to Kate Kilalea and Aniqah Adamjee, whose tireless image research made this book possible. Thanks also to Aaron Walker, without whom none of this would have been feasible.

Raven Smith
2008

COLOPHON

© 2008 Black Dog Publishing Limited, London, UK, and the author. All rights reserved.

Black Dog Publishing Limited
10A Acton Street
London WC1X 9NG
United Kingdom

Tel: +44 (0) 20 7713 5097
Fax: +44 (0) 20 7713 8682
info@blackdogonline.com
www.blackdogonline.com

British Library Cataloguing-in-Publication Data.

A CIP record for this book is available from the British Library.

ISBN: 978 1 906155 40 7

Editor: Raven Smith at Black Dog Publishing.

Designer: Julia Trudeau Rivest at Black Dog Publishing.

Text: Susan Mossman at the Science Museum, London.

Black Dog Publishing Limited, London, UK, is an environmentally responsible company. *Fantastic Plastic* is printed on Arctic Gloss, an FSC certified paper.

architecture art design
fashion history photography
theory and things

black dog
publishing

www.blackdogonline.com   london uk